Charles Dickens

The Uncommercial Traveller

Charles Dickens

The Uncommercial Traveller

ISBN/EAN: 9783743314078

Manufactured in Europe, USA, Canada, Australia, Japa

Cover: Foto ©ninafisch / pixelio.de

Manufactured and distributed by brebook publishing software (www.brebook.com)

Charles Dickens

The Uncommercial Traveller

THE
UNCOMMERCIAL TRAVELLER

BY
CHARLES DICKENS.

LONDON:
CHAPMAN AND HALL, 193, PICCADILLY.
MDCCCLXI.

PREFACE.

These papers have been received with very great favour by the Public, and are here reprinted in a convenient form. The Series is, for the time, complete; but it is the Uncommercial Traveller's intention to take to the road again before another winter sets in.

December, 1860.

CONTENTS.

		PAGE
I.—His General Line of Business	. . . .	1
II.—The Shipwreck	. . . . . .	3
III.—Wapping Workhouse	. . . . .	23
IV.—Two Views of a Cheap Theatre	. . .	40
V.—Poor Mercantile Jack	. . . .	57
VI.—Refreshments for Travellers	. . .	76
VII.—Travelling Abroad	. . . . .	89
VIII.—The Great Tasmania's Cargo	. . .	107
IX.—City of London Churches	. . . .	121
X.—Shy Neighbourhoods	. . . . .	137
XI.—Tramps	. . . .	152
XII.—Dullborough Town	. . . . .	170
XIII.—Night Walks	. . . . . .	186
XIV.—Chambers	. . . . . .	200
XV.—Nurse's Stories	. . . . .	219
XVI.—Arcadian London	. . . . .	236
XVII.—The Italian Prisoner	. . . .	250

THE UNCOMMERCIAL TRAVELLER.

I.

HIS GENERAL LINE OF BUSINESS.

Allow me to introduce myself—first negatively.

No landlord is my friend and brother, no chambermaid loves me, no waiter worships me, no boots admires and envies me. No round of beef or tongue or ham is expressly cooked for me, no pigeon-pie is especially made for me, no hotel-advertisement is personally addressed to me, no hotel-room tapestried with great-coats and railway wrappers is set apart for me, no house of public entertainment in the United Kingdom greatly cares for my opinion of its brandy or sherry. When I go upon my journeys, I am not usually rated at a low figure in the bill; when I come home from my journeys, I never get any commission. I know nothing about prices, and should have no idea, if I were put to it, how to wheedle a man into ordering something he doesn't want. As a town traveller, I am never to be seen driving a vehicle externally like a young and volatile pianoforte van, and internally like an oven in which a number of flat boxes are baking in layers. As a country traveller, I am rarely to be found in a gig, and am never to be encountered by a pleasure train, waiting on the platform of a branch station, quite a Druid in the midst of a light Stonehenge of samples.

And yet—proceeding now, to introduce myself positively—I am both a town traveller and a country traveller, and am always on the road. Figuratively speaking, I travel for the great house of Human Interest Brothers, and have rather a large connexion in the fancy goods way. Literally speaking, I am always wandering here and there from my rooms in Covent-garden, London—now about the city streets: now, about the country bye-roads—seeing many little things, and some great things, which, because they interest me, I think may interest others.

These are my brief credentials as the Uncommercial Traveller.

II.

THE SHIPWRECK.

Never had I seen a year going out, or going on, under quieter circumstances. Eighteen hundred and fifty-nine had but another day to live, and truly its end was Peace on that sea-shore that morning.

So settled and orderly was everything seaward, in the bright light of the sun and under the transparent shadows of the clouds, that it was hard to imagine the bay otherwise, for years past or to come, than it was that very day. The Tug-steamer lying a little off the shore, the Lighter lying still nearer to the shore, the boat alongside the Lighter, the regularly turning windlass aboard the Lighter, the methodical figures at work, all slowly and regularly heaving up and down with the breathing of the sea, all seemed as much a part of the nature of the place as the tide itself. The tide was on the flow, and had been for some two hours and a half; there was a slight obstruction in the sea within a few yards of my feet: as if the stump of a tree, with earth enough about it to keep it from lying horizontally on the water, had slipped a little from the land—and as I stood upon the beach and observed it dimpling the light swell that was coming in, I cast a stone over it.

So orderly, so quiet, so regular—the rising and falling of the Tug-steamer, the Lighter, and the boat—the turning of the windlass—the coming in of the tide—that I myself seemed, to my own thinking, anything but new to the spot. Yet, I had never seen it in my life, a minute before, and had traversed two hundred miles to get at it. That very morning I had come bowling down, and struggling up, hill-country roads; looking back at snowy summits; meeting courteous peasants, well to do, driving fat pigs and cattle to market; noting the neat and thrifty dwellings, with their unusual quantity of clean white linen, drying on the bushes; having windy weather suggested by every cotter's little rick, with its thatched straw-ridged and extra straw-ridged into overlapping compartments, like the back of a rhinoceros. Had I not given a lift of fourteen miles to the Coast-Guardsman (kit and all), who was coming to his spell of duty there, and had we not just now parted company? So it was; but the journey seemed to glide down into the placid sea, with other chafe and trouble, and for the moment nothing was so calmly and monotonously real under the sunlight as the gentle rising and falling of the water with its freight, the regular turning of the windlass aboard the Lighter, and the slight obstruction so very near my feet.

O reader, haply turning this page by the fireside at Home and hearing the night wind rumble in the chimney, that slight obstruction was the uppermost fragment of the Wreck of the Royal Charter, Australian trader and passenger ship, Homeward bound, that struck here on the terrible morning of the twenty-sixth of this October, broke into three parts, went down with her treasure of at least five hundred human lives, and has never stirred since!

From which point, or from which, she drove ashore, stern foremost; on which side, or on which, she passed the little Island in the bay, for ages henceforth to be aground certain yards outside her; these are rendered bootless questions by the darkness of that night and the darkness of death. Here she went down.

Even as I stood on the beach, with the words "Here she went down!" in my ears, a diver in his grotesque dress, dipped heavily over the side of the boat alongside the Lighter, and dropped to the bottom. On the shore by the water's edge, was a rough tent, made of fragments of wreck, where other divers and workmen sheltered themselves, and where they had kept Christmas-day with rum and roast beef, to the destruction of their frail chimney. Cast up among the stones and boulders of the beach, were great spars of the lost vessel, and masses of iron twisted by the fury of the sea into the strangest forms. The timber was already bleached and iron rusted, and even these objects did no violence to the prevailing air the whole scene wore, of having been exactly the same for years and years.

Yet, only two short months had gone, since a man, living on the nearest hill-top overlooking the sea, being blown out of bed at about daybreak by the wind that had begun to strip his roof off, and getting upon a ladder with his nearest neighbour to construct some temporary device for keeping his house over his head, saw from the ladder's elevation as he looked down by chance towards the shore, some dark troubled object close in with the land. And he and the other, descending to the beach, and finding the sea mercilessly beating over a great broken ship, had clambered up the stony ways, like staircases without stairs, on which the wild village hangs in little clusters, as fruit hangs on boughs, and had given the alarm. And so, over the hill-slopes, and past the waterfall, and down the gullies where the land drains off into the ocean, the scattered quarrymen and fishermen inhabiting that part of Wales had come running to the dismal sight—their clergyman among them. And as they stood in the leaden morning, stricken with pity, leaning hard against the wind, their breath and vision often failing as the sleet and spray rushed at them from the ever forming and dissolving mountains of sea, and as the wool which was a part of the vessel's cargo blew in with the salt foam and remained upon the land when the foam melted, they saw the ship's life-boat put off from one of the heaps of wreck; and first, there were three men in her, and in a moment she capsized, and there were but two; and again, she was struck by a vast mass of water, and there was but one; and again, she was thrown bottom upward, and that one, with his arm struck through the broken planks and waving as if for the help that could never reach him, went down into the deep.

It was the clergyman himself from whom I heard this, while I stood on the shore, looking in his kind wholesome face as it turned to the spot where the boat had been. The divers were down then, and busy. They were "lifting" to-day, the gold found yesterday—some five-and-twenty thousand pounds. Of three hundred and fifty thousand pounds' worth of gold, three hundred thousand pounds' worth, in round numbers, was at that time recovered. The great bulk of the remainder was surely and steadily coming up. Some loss of sovereigns there would be, of course; indeed, at first sovereigns had drifted in with the sand, and been scattered far and wide over the beach, like sea-shells; but most other golden treasure would be found. As it was brought up, it went aboard the Tug steamer, where good account was taken of it. So tremendous had the force of the sea been when it broke the ship, that it had beaten one great ingot of gold, deep into a strong and heavy piece of her solid ironwork: in which, also, several loose sovereigns that the ingot had swept in before it, had been found, as firmly embedded as though the iron had been liquid when they were forced there. It had been remarked of such bodies come ashore, too, as had been seen by scientific men, that they had been stunned to death, and not suffocated. Observation, both of the internal change that had been wrought in them, and of their external expression, showed death to have been thus merciful and easy. The report was brought, while I was holding such discourse on the beach, that no more bodies had come ashore since last night. It began to be very doubtful whether many more would be thrown up, until the north-east winds of the early spring set in. Moreover, a great number of the passengers, and particularly the second-class women-passengers, were known to have been in the middle of the ship when she parted, and thus the collapsing wreck would have fallen upon them after yawning open, and would keep them down. A diver made known, even then, that he had come upon the body of a man, and had sought to release it from a great superincumbent weight; but that, finding he could not do so without mutilating the remains, he had left it where it was.

It was the kind and wholesome face I have made mention of as being then beside me, that I had purposed to myself to see, when I left home for Wales. I had heard of that clergyman, as having buried many scores of the shipwrecked people; of his having opened his house and heart to their agonised friends; of his having used a most sweet and patient diligence for weeks and weeks, in the performance of the forlornest offices that Man can render to his kind; of his having most tenderly and thoroughly devoted himself to the dead, and to those who were sorrowing for the dead. I had said to myself, "In the Christmas season of the year, I should like to see that man!" And he had swung the gate of his little garden in coming out to meet me, not half an hour ago.

So cheerful of spirit, and guiltless of affectation, as true practical Christianity ever is! I read more of the New Testament in the fresh frank face going up the village beside me, in five minutes, than I have read in anathematising discourses (albeit put to press with enormous flourishing of trumpets), in all my life. I heard more of the Sacred Book in the cordial voice that had nothing to say about its owner, than in all the would-be celestial pairs of bellows that have ever blown conceit at me.

We climbed towards the little church, at a cheery

pace, among the loose stones, the deep mud, the wet coarse grass, the outlying water, and other obstructions from which frost and snow had lately thawed. It was a mistake (my friend was glad to tell me, on the way) to suppose that the peasantry had shown any superstitious avoidance of the drowned; on the whole, they had done very well, and had assisted readily. Ten shillings had been paid for the bringing of each body up to the church, but the way was steep, and a horse and cart (in which it was wrapped in a sheet) were necessary, and three or four men, and, all things considered, it was not a great price. The people were none the richer for the wreck, for it was the season of the herring-shoal—and who could cast nets for fish, and find dead men and women in the draught?

He had the church keys in his hand, and opened the churchyard gate, and opened the church door; and we went in.

It is a little church of great antiquity; there is reason to believe that some church has occupied the spot, these thousand years or more. The pulpit was gone, and other things usually belonging to the church were gone, owing to its living congregation having deserted it for the neighbouring schoolroom, and yielded it up to the dead. The very Commandments had been shouldered out of their places, in the bringing in of the dead; the black wooden tables on which they were painted, were askew, and on the stone pavement below them, and on the stone pavement all over the church, were the marks and stains where the drowned had been laid down. The eye, with little or no aid from the imagination, could yet see how the bodies had been turned, and where the head had been and where the feet. Some faded traces of the wreck of the Australian ship may be discernible on the stone pavement of this little church, hundreds of years hence, when the digging for gold in Australia shall have long and long ceased out of the land.

Forty-four shipwrecked men and women lay here at one time, awaiting burial. Here, with weeping and wailing in every room of his house, my companion worked alone for hours, solemnly surrounded by eyes that could not see him, and by lips that could not speak to him, patiently examining the tattered clothing, cutting off buttons, hair, marks from linen, anything that might lead to subsequent identification, studying faces, looking for a scar, a bent finger, a crooked toe, comparing letters sent to him with the ruin about him. "My dearest brother had bright grey eyes and a pleasant smile," one sister wrote. O poor sister! well for you to be far from here, and keep that as your last remembrance of him!

The ladies of the clergyman's family, his wife and two sisters-in-law, came in among the bodies often. It grew to be the business of their lives to do so. Any new arrival of a bereaved woman would stimulate their pity to compare the description brought, with the dread realities. Sometimes, they would go back, able to say, "I have found him," or, "I think she lies there." Perhaps, the mourner, unable to bear the sight of all that lay in the church, would be led in blindfold. Conducted to the spot with many compassionate words, and encouraged to look, she would say, with a piercing cry, "This is my boy!" and drop insensible on the insensible figure.

He soon observed that in some cases of women, the identification of persons, though complete, was quite at variance with the marks upon the linen; this led him to notice that even the marks upon the linen were sometimes inconsistent with one another; and thus he came to understand that they had dressed in great haste and agitation, and that their clothes had become mixed together. The identification of men by their dress, was rendered extremely difficult, in consequence of a large proportion of them being dressed alike—in clothes of one kind, that is to say supplied by slopsellers and outfitters, and not made by single garments but by hundreds. Many of the men were bringing over parrots, and had receipts upon them for the price of the birds; others had bills of exchange in their pockets, or in belts. Some of these documents, carefully unwrinkled and dried, were little less fresh in appearance that day, than the present page will be under ordinary circumstances, after having been opened three or four times.

In that lonely place, it had not been easy to obtain even such common commodities in towns, as ordinary disinfectants. Pitch had been burnt in the church, as the readiest thing at hand, and the frying-pan in which it had bubbled over a brazier of coals was still there, with its ashes. Hard by the Communion-Table, were some boots that had been taken off the drowned and preserved—a gold-digger's boot, cut down the leg for its removal—a trodden-down man's ankle-boot with a buff cloth top—and others—soaked and sandy, weedy and salt.

From the church, we passed out into the churchyard.

Here, there lay, at that time, one hundred and forty-five bodies, that had come ashore from the wreck. He had buried them, when not identified, in graves containing four each. He had numbered each body in a register describing it, and had placed a corresponding number on each coffin, and over each grave. Identified bodies he had buried singly, in private graves, in another part of the churchyard. Several bodies had been exhumed from the graves of four, as relatives had come from a distance and seen his register; and, when recognised, these have been reburied in private graves, so that the mourners might erect separate headstones over the remains. In all such cases he had performed the funeral service a second time, and the ladies of his house had attended. There had been no offence in the poor ashes when they were brought again to the light of day; the beneficent Earth had already absorbed it. The drowned were buried in their clothes. To supply the great sudden demand for coffins, he had got all the neighbouring people handy at tools, to work the livelong day, and Sunday likewise. The coffins were neatly formed;—I had seen two, waiting for occupants, under the lee of the ruined walls of a stone hut on the beach, within call of the tent where the Christmas Feast was held. Similarly, one of the graves for four was lying open and ready, here, in the churchyard. So much of the scanty space was already devoted to the wrecked people, that the villagers had begun to express uneasy doubts whether they themselves could lie in their own ground, with their forefathers and descendants, by-and-by. The churchyard being but a step from the clergyman's dwelling-house, we crossed to the latter; the white surplice was hanging up near the door ready to be put on at any time, for a funeral service.

The cheerful earnestness of this good Christian minister was as consolatory, as the circumstances out of which it shone were sad. I never have seen anything more delightfully genuine than the calm dismissal by himself and his household of all they had undergone, as a simple duty that was quietly done and ended. In speaking of it, they spoke of it with great compassion for the bereaved; but laid no stress upon their own hard share in those weary weeks, except as it had attached many people to them as friends, and elicited many touching expressions of gratitude. This clergyman's brother—himself the clergyman of two adjoining parishes, who had buried thirty-four of the bodies in his own churchyard, and who had done to them all that his brother had done as to the larger number—must be understood as included in the family. He was there, with his neatly arranged papers, and made no more account of his trouble than anybody else did. Down to yesterday's post outward, my clergyman alone had written one thousand and seventy-five letters to relatives and friends of the lost people. In the absence of self-assertion, it was only through my now and then delicately putting a question as the occasion arose, that I became informed of these things. It was only when I had remarked again and again, in the church, on the awful nature of the scene of death he had been required so closely to familiarise himself with for the soothing of the living, that he had casually said, without the least abatement of his cheerfulness, "indeed, it had rendered him unable for a time to eat or drink more than a little coffee now and then, and a piece of bread."

In this noble modesty, in this beautiful simplicity, in this serene avoidance of the least attempt to "improve" an occasion which might be supposed to have sunk of its own weight into my heart, I seemed to have happily come, in a few steps, from the churchyard with its open grave, which was the type of Death, to the Christian dwelling side by side with it, which was the type of Resurrection. I never shall think of the former, without the latter. The two will always rest side by side in my memory. If I had lost any one dear to me in this unfortunate ship, if I had made a voyage from Australia to look at the grave in the churchyard, I should go away, thankful to God that that house was so close to it, and that its shadow by day and its domestic lights by night fell upon the earth in which its Master had so tenderly laid my dear one's head.

The references that naturally arose out of our conversation, to the descriptions sent down of shipwrecked persons, and to the gratitude of relations and friends, made me very anxious to see some of those letters. I was presently seated before a shipwreck of papers, all bordered with black, and from them I made the following few extracts.

A mother writes:

Reverend Sir. Amongst the many who perished on your shore was numbered my beloved son. I was only just recovering from a severe illness, and this fearful affliction has caused a relapse, so that I am unable at present to go to identify the remains of the loved and lost. My darling son would have been sixteen on Christmas-day next. He was a most amiable and obedient child, early taught the way of salvation. We fondly hoped that as a British seaman he might be an ornament to his profession, but, "it is well;" I feel assured my dear boy is now with the redeemed. Oh, he did not wish to go this last voyage! On the fifteenth of October, I received a letter from him from Melbourne, date August twelfth; he wrote in high spirits, and in conclusion he says; "Pray for a fair breeze, dear mamma, and I'll not forget to whistle for it! and, God permitting, I shall see you and all my little pets again. Good-by, dear mother—good-by, dearest parents. Good-by, dear brother." Oh, it was indeed an eternal farewell. I do not apologise for thus writing you, for oh, my heart is so very sorrowful.

A husband writes:

My dear kind Sir. Will you kindly inform me whether there are any initials upon the ring and guard you have in possession, found, as the Standard says, last Tuesday? Believe me, my dear sir, when I say that I cannot express my deep gratitude in words sufficiently for your kindness to me on that fearful and appalling day. Will you tell me what I can do for you, and will you write me a consoling letter to prevent my mind from going astray?

A widow writes:

Left in such a state as I am, my friends and I thought it best that my dear husband should be buried where he lies, and, much as I should have liked to have had it otherwise, I must submit. I feel, from all I have heard of you, that you will see it done decently and in order. Little does it signify to us, when the soul has departed, where this poor body lies, but we who are left behind would do all we can to show how we loved them. This is denied me, but it is God's hand that afflicts us, and I try to submit. Some day I may be able to visit the spot, and see where he lies, and erect a simple stone to his memory. Oh! it will be long, long before I forget that dreadful night! Is there such a thing in the vicinity, or any shop in Bangor, to which I could send for a small picture of Moelfra or Llanallgo church, a spot now sacred to me?

Another widow writes:

I have received your letter this morning, and do thank you most kindly for the interest you have taken about my dear husband, as well for the sentiments yours contains, evincing the spirit of a Christian who can sympathise with those who, like myself, are broken down with grief.

May God bless and sustain you, and all in connexion with you, in this great trial. Time may roll on and bear all its sons away, but your name as a disinterested person will stand in history, and, as successive years pass, many a widow will think of your noble conduct, and the tears of gratitude flow down many a cheek, the tribute of a thankful heart, when other things are forgotten for ever.

A father writes:

I am at a loss to find words to sufficiently express my gratitude to you for your kindness to my son Richard upon the melancholy occasion of his visit to his dear brother's body, and also for your ready attention in pronouncing our beautiful burial service over my poor unfortunate son's remains. God grant that your prayers over him may reach the Mercy Seat, and that his soul may be received (through Christ's intercession) into heaven!

His dear mother begs me to convey to you her heartfelt thanks.

Those who were received at the clergyman's house, write thus, after leaving it:

DEAR AND NEVER-TO-BE-FORGOTTEN FRIENDS. I arrived here yesterday morning without accident, and am about to proceed to my home by railway.

I am overpowered when I think of you and your hospitable home. No words could speak language suited to my heart. I refrain. God reward you with the same measure you have meted with!

I enumerate no names, but embrace you all.

My beloved Friends. This is the first day that I have been able to leave my bedroom since I returned, which will explain the reason of my not writing sooner.

If I could only have had my last melancholy hope realised in recovering the body of my beloved and lamented son, I should have returned home somewhat comforted, and I think I could then have been comparatively resigned.

I fear now there is but little prospect, and I mourn as one without hope.

The only consolation to my distressed mind is in having been so feelingly allowed by you to leave the matter in your hands, by whom I well know that everything will be done that can be, according to arrangements made before I left the scene of the awful catastrophe, both as to the identification of my dear son, and also his interment.

I feel most anxious to hear whether anything fresh has transpired since I left you; will you add another to the many deep obligations I am under to you by writing to me? And, should the body of my dear and unfortunate son be identified, let me hear from you immediately, and I will come again.

Words cannot express the gratitude I feel I owe to you all for your benevolent aid, your kindness, and your sympathy.

My dearly beloved Friends. I arrived in safety at my house yesterday, and a night's rest has restored and tranquillised me. I must again repeat, that language has no words by which I can express my sense of obligation to you You are enshrined in my heart of hearts.

C

I have seen him! and can now realise my misfortune more than I have hitherto been able to do. Oh, the bitterness of the cup I drink! But I bow submissive. God *must* have done right. I do not want to feel less, but to acquiesce more simply.

There were some Jewish passengers on board the Royal Charter, and the gratitude of the Jewish people is feelingly expressed in the following letter, bearing date from "the office of the Chief Rabbi:"

Reverend Sir. I cannot refrain from expressing to you my heartfelt thanks on behalf of those of my flock whose relatives have unfortunately been among those who perished at the late wreck of the Royal Charter. You have, indeed, like Boaz, "not left off your kindness to the living and the dead."

You have not alone acted kindly towards the living by receiving them hospitably at your house, and energetically assisting them in their mournful duty, but also towards the dead, by exerting yourself to have our co-religionists buried in our ground, and according to our rites. May our heavenly Father reward you for your acts of humanity and true philanthropy!

The "Old Hebrew congregation of Liverpool" thus express themselves through their secretary:

Reverend Sir. The wardens of this congregation have learned with great pleasure that, in addition to those indefatigable exertions, at the scene of the late disaster to the Royal Charter, which have received universal recognition, you have very benevolently employed your valuable efforts to assist such members of our faith as have sought the bodies of lost friends to give them burial in our consecrated grounds, with the observances and rites prescribed by the ordinances of our religion.

The wardens desire me to take the earliest available opportunity to offer to you, on behalf of our community, the expression of their warm acknowledgments and grateful thanks, and their sincere wishes for your continued welfare and prosperity.

A Jewish gentleman writes:

REVEREND AND DEAR SIR. I take the opportunity of thanking you right earnestly for the promptness you displayed in answering my note with full particulars concerning my much-lamented brother, and I also herein beg to express my sincere regard for the willingness you displayed and for the facility you afforded for getting the remains of my poor brother exhumed. It has been to us a most sorrowful and painful event, but when we meet with such friends as yourself, it in a measure, somehow or other, abates that mental anguish, and makes the suffering so much easier to be borne. Considering the circumstances connected with my poor brother's fate, it does, indeed, appear a hard one. He had been away in all seven years; he returned four years ago to see his family. He was then engaged to a very amiable young lady. He had been very successful abroad, and was now returning to fulfil his sacred vow; he brought all his property with him in gold uninsured. We heard from him when the ship stopped at Queenstown, when he was in the highest of hope, and in a few short hours afterwards all was washed away.

Mournful in the deepest degree, but too sacred for quotation here, were the numerous references to those miniatures of women worn round the necks of rough men (and found there after death), those locks of hair, those scraps of letters, those many many slight memorials of hidden tenderness. One man cast up by the sea bore about him, printed on a perforated lace card, the following singular (and unavailing) charm :

A BLESSING.

May the blessing of God await thee. May the sun of glory shine around thy bed ; and may the gates of plenty, honour, and happiness be ever open to thee. May no sorrow distress thy days ; may no grief disturb thy nights. May the pillow of peace kiss thy cheek, and the pleasures of imagination attend thy dreams ; and when length of years makes thee tired of earthly joys, and the curtain of death gently closes around thy last sleep of human existence, may the Angel of God attend thy bed, and take care that the expiring lamp of life shall not receive one rude blast to hasten on its extinction.

A sailor had these devices on his right arm. "Our Saviour on the Cross, the forehead of the Crucifix and the vesture stained red; on the lower part of the arm, a man and woman ; on one side of the Cross, the appearance of a half moon, with a face; on the other side, the sun ; on the top of the Cross, the letters I.H.S.; on the left arm, a man and woman dancing, with an effort to delineate the female's dress ; under which, initials." Another seaman "had, on the lower part of the right arm, the device of a sailor and a female; the man holding the Union Jack with a streamer, the folds of which waved over her head, and the end of it was held in her hand. On the upper part of the arm, a device of Our Lord on the Cross, with stars surrounding the head of the Cross, and one large star on the side in Indian ink. On the left arm, a flag, a true lovers' knot, a face, and initials." This tattooing was found still plain, below the discoloured outer surface of a mutilated arm, when such surface was carefully scraped away with a knife. It is not improbable that the perpetuation of this marking custom among seamen, may be referred back to their desire to be identified, if drowned and flung ashore.

It was some time before I could sever myself from the many interesting papers on the table, and then I broke bread and drank wine with the kind family before I left them. As I brought the Coast-guard down, so I took the Postman back, with his leathern wallet, walking-stick, bugle, and terrier dog. Many a heart-broken letter had he brought to the Rectory House within two months; many a benignantly painstaking answer had he carried back.

As I rode along, I thought of the many people, inhabitants of this mother country, who would make pilgrimages to the little churchyard in the years to come; I thought of the many people in Australia, who would have an interest in such a shipwreck, and would find their way here when they visit the Old World; I thought of the writers of all the wreck of letters I had left upon the table; and I resolved to place this little record where it stands. Convocations, Conferences, Diocesan Epistles, and the like, will do a great deal for Religion, I dare say, and Heaven send they may! but I doubt if they will ever do their Master's service half so well, in all the time they last, as the Heavens have seen it done in this bleak spot upon the rugged coast of Wales.

Had I lost the friend of my life, in the wreck of the

Royal Charter; had I lost my betrothed, the more than friend of my life; had I lost my maiden daughter, had I lost my hopeful boy, had I lost my little child; I would kiss the hands that worked so busily and gently in the church, and say, "None better could have touched the form, though it had lain at home." I could be sure of it, I could be thankful for it: I could be content to leave the grave near the house the good family pass in and out of every day, undisturbed, in the little churchyard where so many are so strangely brought together.

Without the name of the clergyman to whom—I hope, not without carrying comfort to some heart at some time —I have referred, my reference would be as nothing. He is the Reverend Stephen Roose Hughes, of Llanallgo, near Moelfra, Anglesey. His brother is the Reverend Hugh Robert Hughes, of Penrhos Alligwy.

III.

WAPPING WORKHOUSE.

My day's no-business beckoning me to the East end of London, I had turned my face to that point of the metropolitan compass on leaving Covent Garden, and had got past the India House, thinking in my idle manner of Tippoo-Sahib and Charles Lamb, and had got past my little wooden midshipman, after affectionately patting him on one leg of his knee-shorts for old acquaintance' sake, and had got past Aldgate Pump, and had got past the Saracen's Head (with an ignominious rash of posting-bills disfiguring his swarthy countenance), and had strolled up the empty yard of his ancient neighbour the Black or Blue Boar, or Bull, who departed this life I don't know when, and whose coaches are all gone I don't know where; and I had come out again into the age of railways, and I had got past Whitechapel Church, and was—rather inappropriately for an Uncommercial Traveller—in the Commercial Road. Pleasantly wallowing in the abundant mud of that thoroughfare, and greatly enjoying the huge piles of building belonging to the sugar refiners, the little masts and vanes in small back gardens in back streets, the neighbouring canals and docks, the India-vans lumbering along their stone tramway, and the pawnbrokers' shops where hard-up Mates had pawned so many sextants and quadrants, that I should have bought a few cheap if I had the least notion how to use them, I at last began to file off to the right, towards Wapping.

Not that I intended to take boat at Wapping Old Stairs, or that I was going to look at the locality, because I believe (for I don't) in the constancy of the young woman who told her sea-going lover, to such a beautiful old tune, that she had ever continued the same, since she gave him the 'baccer-box marked with his name; I am afraid he usually got the worst of those transactions, and was frightfully taken in. No, I was going to Wapping, because an Eastern police magistrate had said, through the morning papers, that there was no classification at the Wapping workhouse for women, and that it was a disgrace and a shame and divers other hard names, and because I wished to see how the fact really stood. For, that Eastern police magistrates are not always the wisest men of the East, may be inferred from their course of procedure respecting the fancy-dressing and pantomime-posturing at St. George's in that quarter: which is usually, to discuss the matter at issue, in a state of mind betokening the weakest perplexity, with all parties concerned and unconcerned, and, for a final expedient, to consult the complainant as to what he thinks ought to be done with the defendant, and take the defendant's opinion as to what he would recommend to be done with himself.

Long before I reached Wapping, I gave myself up as having lost my way, and, abandoning myself to the narrow streets in a Turkish frame of mind, relied on predestination to bring me somehow or other to the place I wanted if I were ever to get there. When I had ceased for an hour or so to take any trouble about the matter, I found myself on a swing-bridge, looking down at some dark locks in some dirty water. Over against me, stood a creature remotely in the likeness of a young man, with a puffed sallow face, and a figure all dirty and shiny and slimy, who may have been the youngest son of his filthy old father, Thames, or the drowned man about whom there was a placard on the granite post like a large thimble, that stood between us.

I asked this apparition what it called the place? Unto which, it replied, with a ghastly grin and a sound like gurgling water in its throat:

"Mister Baker's trap."

As it is a point of great sensitiveness with me on such occasions to be equal to the intellectual pressure of the conversation, I deeply considered the meaning of this speech, while I eyed the apparition—then engaged in hugging and sucking a horizontal iron bar at the top of the locks. Inspiration suggested to me that Mr. Baker was the acting Coroner of that neighbourhood.

"A common place for suicide," said I, looking down at the locks.

"Sue?" returned the ghost, with a stare. "Yes! And Poll. Likeways Emly. And Nancy. And Jane;" he sucked the iron between each name; "and all the bileing. Ketches off their bonnets or shorls, takes a run, and headers down here, they does. Always a headerin' down here, they is. Like one o'clock."

"And at about that hour of the morning, I suppose?"

"Ah!" said the apparition. "*They* an't partickler. Two 'ull do for *them*. Three. All times o' night. O'ny mind you!" Here the apparition rested his profile on the bar, and gurgled in a sarcastic manner. "There must be somebody comin'. They don't go a headerin' down here, wen there an't no Bobby nor gen'ral Cove, fur to hear the splash."

According to my interpretation of these words, I was myself a General Cove, or member of the miscellaneous public. In which modest character, I remarked:

"They are often taken out, are they, and restored?"

"I dunno about restored," said the apparition, who, for some occult reason, very much objected to that word; "they're carried into the werkiss and put into a 'ot bath, and brought round. But I dunno about restored," said the apparition; "blow *that!*"—and vanished.

As it had shown a desire to become offensive, I was not sorry to find myself alone, especially as the "werkiss" it had indicated with a twist of its matted head, was close at hand. So I left Mr. Baker's terrible trap (baited with a scum that was like the soapy rinsing of sooty chimneys), and made bold to ring at the workhouse gate, where I was wholly unexpected and quite unknown.

A very bright and nimble little matron, with a bunch of keys in her hand, responded to my request to see the House. I began to doubt whether the police magistrate was quite right in his facts, when I noticed her quick active little figure and her intelligent eyes.

The Traveller (the matron intimated) should see the worst first. He was welcome to see everything. Such as it was, there it all was.

This was the only preparation for our entering "the Foul wards." They were in an old building squeezed away in a corner of a paved yard, quite detached from the more modern and spacious main body of the workhouse. They were in a building most monstrously behind the time—a mere series of garrets or lofts, with every inconvenient and objectionable circumstance in their construction, and only accessible by steep and narrow staircases, infamously ill adapted for the passage up-stairs of the sick or down stairs of the dead.

A-bed in these miserable rooms, here on bedsteads, there (for a change, as I understood it) on the floor, were women in every stage of distress and disease. None but those who have attentively observed such scenes, can conceive the extraordinary variety of expression still latent under the general monotony and uniformity of colour, attitude, and condition. The form a little coiled up and turned away, as though it had turned its back on this world for ever; the uninterested face at once lead-coloured and yellow, looking passively upward from the pillow; the haggard mouth a little dropped, the hand outside the coverlet, so dull and indifferent, so light, and yet so heavy; these were on every pallet; but, when I stopped beside a bed, and said ever so slight a word to the figure lying there, the ghost of the old character came into the face, and made the Foul ward as various as the fair world. No one appeared to care to live, but no one complained; all who could speak, said that as much was done for them as could be done there, that the attendance was kind and patient, that their suffering was very heavy, but they had nothing to ask for. The wretched rooms were as clean and sweet as it is possible for such rooms to be; they would become a pest-house in a single week, if they were ill-kept.

I accompanied the brisk matron up another barbarous staircase, into a better kind of loft devoted to the idiotic and imbecile. There was at least Light in it, whereas the windows in the former wards had been like sides of schoolboys' birdcages. There was a strong grating over the fire here, and, holding a kind of state on either side of the hearth, separated by the breadth of this grating, were two old ladies in a condition of feeble dignity, which was surely the very last and lowest reduction of self-complacency, to be found in this wonderful humanity of ours. They were evidently jealous of each other, and passed their whole time (as some people do, whose fires are not grated) in mentally disparaging each other, and contemptuously watching their neighbours. One of these parodies on provincial gentlewomen was extremely talkative, and expressed a strong desire to attend the service on Sundays, from which she represented herself to have derived the greatest interest and consolation when allowed that privilege. She gossiped so well, and looked altogether so cheery and harmless, that I began to think this a case for the Eastern magistrate, until I found that on the last occasion of her attending chapel, she had secreted a small stick, and had caused some confusion in the responses by suddenly producing it and belabouring the congregation.

So, these two old ladies, separated by the breadth of the grating—otherwise they would fly at one another's caps—sat all day long, suspecting one another, and contemplating a world of fits. For, everybody else in the room had fits, except the wardswoman; an elderly, ablebodied pauperess, with a large upper lip, and an air of repressing and saving her strength, as she stood with her hands folded before her, and her eyes slowly rolling, biding her time for catching or holding somebody. This civil personage (in whom I regretted to identify a reduced member of my honourable friend Mrs. Gamp's family) said, "They has 'em continiwal, sir. They drops without no more notice than if they was coach-horses dropped from the moon, sir. And when one drops, another drops, and sometimes there'll be as many as four or five on 'em at once, dear me, a rollin' and a tearin', bless you!—this young woman, now, has 'em dreadful bad."

She turned up this young woman's face with her hand as she said it. This young woman was seated on the floor, pondering, in the foreground of the afflicted. There was nothing repellant, either in her face or head. Many, apparently worse, varieties of epilepsy and hysteria were about her, but she was said to be the worst there. When

I had spoken to her a little, she still sat with her face turned up, pondering, and a gleam of the mid-day sun shone in upon her.

—Whether this young woman, and the rest of these so sorely troubled, as they sit or lie pondering in their confused dull way, ever get mental glimpses among the motes in the sunlight, of healthy people and healthy things? Whether this young woman, brooding like this in the summer season, ever thinks that somewhere there are trees and flowers, even mountains and the great sea? Whether, not to go so far, this young woman ever has any dim revelation of that young woman—that young woman who is not here and never will come here; who is courted, and caressed, and loved, and has a husband, and bears children, and lives in a home, and who never knows what it is to have this lashing and tearing coming upon her? And whether this young woman, God help her, gives herself up then and drops, like a coach-horse from the moon?

I hardly knew whether the voices of infant children, penetrating into so hopeless a place, made a sound that was pleasant or painful to me. It was something to be reminded that the weary world was not all aweary, and was ever renewing itself; but, this young woman was a child not long ago, and a child not long hence might be such as she. Howbeit, the active step and eye of the vigilant matron conducted me past the two provincial gentlewomen (whose dignity was ruffled by the children), and into the adjacent nursery.

There were many babies here, and more than one handsome young mother. There were ugly young mothers also, and sullen young mothers, and callous young mothers. But, the babies had not appropriated to themselves any bad expression yet, and might have been, for anything that appeared to the contrary in their soft faces, Princes Imperial, and Princesses Royal. I had the pleasure of giving a poetical commission to the baker's man to make a cake with all despatch and toss it into the oven for one red-headed young pauper and myself, and felt much the better for it. Without that refreshment, I doubt if I should have been in a condition for "the Refractories," towards whom my quick little matron—for whose adaptation to her office I had by this time conceived a genuine respect—drew me next, and marshalled me the way that I was going.

The Refractories were picking oakum, in a small room giving on a yard. They sat in line on a form, with their backs to a window; before them, a table, and their work. The oldest Refractory was, say twenty; youngest Refractory, say sixteen. I have never yet ascertained, in the course of my uncommercial travels, why a Refractory habit should affect the tonsils and uvula; but, I have always observed that Refractories of both sexes and every grade, between a Ragged School and the Old Bailey, have one voice, in which the tonsils and uvula gain a diseased ascendancy.

"Five pound indeed! I hain't a going fur to pick five pound," said the Chief of the Refractories, keeping time to herself with her head and chin. "More than enough to pick what we picks now, in sitch a place as this, and on wot we gets here!"

(This was in acknowledgment of a delicate intimation that the amount of work was likely to be increased. It certainly was not heavy then, for one Refractory had already done her day's task—it was barely two o'clock—and was sitting behind it, with a head exactly matching it.)

"A pretty Ouse this is, matron, ain't it?" said Refractory Two, "where a pleeseman's called in, if a gal says a word!"

"And wen you're sent to prison for nothink or less!" said the Chief, tugging at her oakum as if it were the matron's hair. "But any place is better than this; that's one thing, and be thankful!"

A laugh of Refractories led by Oakum Head with folded arms—who originated nothing, but who was in command of the skirmishers outside the conversation.

"If any place is better than this," said my brisk guide, in the calmest manner, "it is a pity you left a good place when you had one."

"Ho, no, I didn't, matron," returned the Chief, with another pull at her oakum, and a very expressive look at the enemy's forehead. "Don't say that, matron, cos it's lies!"

Oakum Head brought up the skirmishers again, skirmished, and retired.

"And *I* warn't a going," exclaimed Refractory Two, "though I was in one place for as long as four year—I warn't a going fur to stop in a place that warn't fit for me—there! And where the fam'ly warn't 'spectable characters—there! And where I fort'nately or hunfort'nately, found that the people warn't what they pretended to make theirselves out to be—there! And where it wasn't their faults, by chalks, if I warn't made bad and ruinated—Hah!"

During this speech, Oakum Head had again made a diversion with the skirmishers, and had again withdrawn.

The Uncommercial Traveller ventured to remark that he supposed Chief Refractory and Number One, to be the two young women who had been taken before the magistrate?

"Yes!" said the Chief, "we har! and the wonder is, that a pleeseman an't 'ad in now, and we took off agen. You can't open your lips here, without a pleeseman."

Number Two laughed (very uvularly), and the skirmishers followed suit.

"I'm sure I'd be thankful," protested the Chief, looking sideways at the Uncommercial, "if I could be got into a place, or got abroad. I'm sick and tired of this precious Ouse, I am, with reason."

So would be, and so was, Number Two. So would be, and so was, Oakum Head. So would be, and so were, Skirmishers.

The Uncommercial took the liberty of hinting that he hardly thought it probable that any lady or gentleman in want of a likely young domestic of retiring manners, would be tempted into the engagement of either of the two leading Refractories, on her own presentation of herself as per sample.

"It ain't no good being nothink else here," said the Chief.

The Uncommercial thought it might be worth trying.

"Oh no it ain't," said the Chief.

"Not a bit of good," said Number Two.

"And I'm sure I'd be very thankful to be got into a place, or got abroad," said the Chief.

"And so should I," said Number Two. "Truly thankful, I should."

Oakum Head then rose, and announced as an entirely new idea, the mention of which profound novelty might be naturally expected to startle her unprepared hearers, that she would be very thankful to be got into a place, or got abroad. And, as if she had then said, "Chorus, ladies!" all the Skirmishers struck up to the same purpose. We left them, thereupon, and began a long walk among the women who were simply old and infirm; but whenever, in the course of this same walk, I looked out of any high window that commanded the yard, I saw Oakum Head and all the other Refractories looking out at their low window for me, and never failing to catch me, the moment I showed my head.

In ten minutes I had ceased to believe in such fables of a golden time as youth, the prime of life, or a hale old age. In ten minutes, all the lights of womankind seemed to have been blown out, and nothing in that way to be left this vault to brag of, but the flickering and expiring snuffs.

And what was very curious, was, that these dim old

women had one company notion which was the fashion of the place. Every old woman who became aware of a visitor and was not in bed, hobbled over a form into her accustomed seat, and became one of a line of dim old women confronting another line of dim old women across a narrow table. There was no obligation whatever upon them to range themselves in this way; it was their manner of "receiving." As a rule, they made no attempt to talk to one another, or to look at the visitor, or to look at anything, but sat silently working their mouths, like a sort of poor old Cows. In some of these wards, it was good to see a few green plants; in others, an isolated Refractory acting as nurse, who did well enough in that capacity, when separated from her compeers; every one of these wards, day room, night room, or both combined, was scrupulously clean and fresh. I have seen as many such places as most travellers in my line, and I never saw one such, better kept.

Among the bedridden there was great patience, great reliance on the books under the pillow, great faith in GOD. All cared for sympathy, but none much cared to be encouraged with hope of recovery; on the whole, I should say, it was considered rather a distinction to have a complication of disorders, and to be in a worse way than the rest. From some of the windows, the river could be seen with all its life and movement; the day was bright, but I came upon no one who was looking out.

In one large ward, sitting by the fire in arm-chairs of distinction, like the President and Vice of the good company, were two old women, upwards of ninety years of age. The younger of the two, just turned ninety, was deaf, but not very, and could easily be made to hear. In her early time she had nursed a child, who was now another old woman, more infirm than herself, inhabiting the very same chamber. She perfectly understood this when the matron told it, and, with sundry nods and motions of her forefinger, pointed out the woman in question. The elder of this pair, ninety-three, seated before an illustrated newspaper (but not reading it), was a bright-eyed old soul, really not deaf, wonderfully preserved, and amazingly conversational. She had not long lost her husband, and had been in that place little more than a year. At Boston, in the State of Massachusetts, this poor creature would have been individually addressed, would have been tended in her own room, and would have had her life gently assimilated to a comfortable life out of doors. Would that be much to do in England for a woman who has kept herself out of a workhouse more than ninety rough long years? When Britain first, at Heaven's command, arose, with a great deal of allegorical confusion, from out the azure main, did her guardian angels positively forbid it in the Charter which has been so much be-snug?

The object of my journey was accomplished when the nimble matron had no more to show me. As I shook hands with her at the gate, I told her that I thought Justice had not used her very well, and that the wise men of the East were not infallible.

Now, I reasoned with myself, as I made my journey home again, concerning those Foul wards. They ought not to exist; no person of common decency and humanity can see them and doubt it. But what is this Union to do? The necessary alteration would cost several thousands of pounds; it has already to support three workhouses; its inhabitants work hard for their bare lives, and are already rated for the relief of the Poor to the utmost extent of reasonable endurance. One poor parish in this very Union is rated to the amount of FIVE AND SIXPENCE in the pound, at the very same time when the rich parish of Saint George's, Hanover-square, is rated at about SEVENPENCE in the pound, Paddington at about FOURPENCE, Saint James's, Westminster, at about TENPENCE! It is only through the equalisation of Poor Rates that what is left undone in this wise, can be done. Much more is left undone, or is ill-done, than I have space to suggest in these notes of a single uncommercial journey; but, the wise men of the East, before they can reasonably hold forth about it, must look to the North and South and West; let them also, any morning before taking the seat of Solomon, look into the shops and dwellings all around the Temple, and first ask themselves "how much more can these poor people—many of whom keep themselves with difficulty enough out of the workhouse—bear?"

I had yet other matter for reflection, as I journeyed home, inasmuch as, before I altogether departed from the neighbourhood of Mr. Baker's trap, I had knocked at the gate of the workhouse of St. George's-in-the-East, and had found it to be an establishment highly creditable to those parts, and thoroughly well administered by a most intelligent master. I remarked in it, an instance of the collateral harm that obstinate vanity and folly can do. "This was the Hall where those old paupers, male and female, whom I had just seen, met for the Church service, was it?"—"Yes."—"Did they sing the Psalms to any instrument?"—"They would like to, very much; they would have an extraordinary interest in doing so." —"And could none be got?"—"Well, a piano could even have been got for nothing, but these unfortunate dissensions——" Ah! better, far better, my Christian friend in the beautiful garment, to have let the singing boys alone, and left the multitude to sing for themselves! You should know better than I, but I think I have read that they did so, once upon a time, and that "when they had sung an hymn," Some one (not in a beautiful garment) went up unto the Mount of Olives.

It made my heart ache to think of this miserable trifling, in the streets of a city where every stone seemed to call to me, as I walked along, "Turn this way, man, and see what waits to be done!" So I decoyed myself into another train of thought to ease my heart. But, I don't know that I did it, for I was so full of paupers, that it was, after all, only a change to a single pauper, who took possession of my remembrance instead of a thousand.

"I beg your pardon, sir," he had said, in a confidential manner, on another occasion, taking me aside; "but I have seen better days."

"I am very sorry to hear it."

"Sir, I have a complaint to make against the master."

"I have no power here, I assure you. And if I had——"

"But allow me, sir, to mention it, as between yourself and a man who has seen better days, sir. The master and myself are both masons, sir, and I make him the sign continually; but, because I am in this unfortunate position, sir, he won't give me the countersign"!

IV.

TWO VIEWS OF A CHEAP THEATRE.

As I shut the door of my lodging behind me, and came out into the streets at six on a drizzling Saturday evening in the last past month of January, all that neighbourhood of Covent-garden looked very desolate. It is so essentially a neighbourhood which has seen better days, that bad weather affects it sooner than another place which has not come down in the world. In its present reduced condition, it bears a thaw almost worse than any place I know. It gets so dreadfully low-spirited, when damp breaks forth. Those wonderful houses about Drury-lane Theatre, which in the palmy days of theatres were prosperous and long-settled places of business, and which now change hands every week, but never change their character of being divided and subdivided on the ground floor into mouldy dens of shops where an orange and half a dozen nuts, or a pomatum-pot, one cake of fancy soap, and a cigar-box, are offered for sale and never sold, were most ruefully contemplated that evening, by the statue of Shakespeare, with the rain-drops coursing one another down its innocent nose. Those inscrutable pigeon-hole offices, with nothing in them (not so much as an inkstand) but a model of a theatre before the curtain, where, in the Italian Opera season, tickets at reduced prices are kept on sale by nomadic gentlemen in smeary hats too tall for them, whom one occasionally seems to have seen on race-courses, not wholly unconnected with strips of cloth of various colours and a rolling ball—those Bedouin establishments, deserted by the tribe, and tenantless except when sheltering in one corner an irregular row of ginger-beer-bottles which would have made one shudder on such a night, but for its being plain that they had nothing in them, shrunk from the shrill cries of the newsboys at their Exchange in the kennel of Catherine-street, like guilty things upon a fearful summons. At the pipe-shop in Great Russell-street, the Death's-head pipes were like theatrical memento mori, admonishing beholders of the decline of the playhouse as an Institution. I walked up Bow-street, disposed to be angry with the shops there, that were letting out theatrical secrets by exhibiting to work-a-day humanity the stuff of which diadems and robes of kings are made. I noticed that some shops which had once been in the dramatic line, and had struggled out of it, were not getting on prosperously—like some actors I have known, who took to business and failed to make it answer. In a word, those streets looked so dull, and, considered as theatrical streets, so broken and bankrupt, that the FOUND DEAD on the black board at the police station might have announced the decease of the Drama, and the pools of water outside the fire-engine maker's at the corner of Long-acre might have been occasioned by his having brought out the whole of his stock to play upon its last smouldering ashes.

And yet, on such a night in so degenerate a time, the object of my journey was theatrical. And yet within half an hour I was in an immense theatre, capable of holding nearly five thousand people.

What Theatre? Her Majesty's? Far better. Royal Italian Opera? Far better. Infinitely superior to the latter for hearing in; infinitely superior to both, for seeing in. To every part of this Theatre, spacious fire-proof ways of ingress and egress. For every part of it, convenient places of refreshment and retiring rooms. Everything to eat and drink carefully supervised as to quality, and sold at an appointed price; respectable female attendants ready for the commonest women in the audience; a general air of consideration, decorum, and supervision, most commendable; an unquestionably humanising influence in all the social arrangements of the place.

Surely a dear Theatre, then? Because there were in London (not very long ago) Theatres with entrance-prices up to half a guinea a head, whose arrangements were not half so civilised. Surely, therefore, a dear Theatre? Not very dear. A gallery at threepence, another gallery at fourpence, a pit at sixpence, boxes and pit-stalls at a shilling, and a few private boxes at half-a-crown.

My uncommercial curiosity induced me to go into every nook of this great place, and among every class of the audience assembled in it—amounting that evening, as I calculated, to about two thousand and odd hundreds. Magnificently lighted by a firmament of sparkling chandeliers, the building was ventilated to perfection. My sense of smell, without being particularly delicate, has been so offended in some of the commoner places of public resort, that I have often been obliged to leave them when I have made an uncommercial journey expressly to look on. The air of this Theatre was fresh, cool, and wholesome. To help towards this end, very sensible precautions had been used, ingeniously combining the experience of hospitals and railway stations. Asphalte pavements substituted for wooden floors, honest bare walls of glazed brick and tile—even at the back of the boxes—for plaster and paper, no benches stuffed, and no carpeting or baize used: a cool material with a light glazed surface, being the covering of the seats.

These various contrivances are as well considered in the place in question as if it were a Fever Hospital; the result is, that it is sweet and healthful. It has been constructed from the ground to the roof, with a careful reference to sight and sound in every corner; the result is, that its form is beautiful, and that the appearance of the audience, as seen from the proscenium—with every face in it commanding the stage, and the whole so admirably raked and turned to that centre, that a hand can scarcely move in the great assemblage without the movement being seen from thence—is highly remarkable in its union of vastness with compactness. The stage itself, and all its appurtenances of machinery, cellarage, height, and breadth, are on a scale more like the Scala at Milan, or the San Carlo at Naples, or the Grand Opera at Paris, than any notion a stranger would be likely to form of the Britannia Theatre at Hoxton, a mile north of St. Luke's Hospital in the Old-street-road, London. The Forty Thieves might be played here, and every thief ride his real horse, and the disguised captain bring in his oil jars on a train of real camels, and nobody be put out of the way. This really extraordinary place is the achievement of one man's enterprise, and was erected on the ruins of an inconvenient old building, in less than five months, at a round cost of five-and-twenty thousand pounds. To dismiss this part of my subject, and still to render to the proprietor the credit that is strictly his due, I must add that his sense of the responsibility upon him to make the best of his audience, and to do his best for them, is a highly agreeable sign of these times.

As the spectators at this theatre, for a reason I will presently show, were the object of my journey, I entered on the play of the night as one of the two thousand and odd hundreds, by looking about me at my neighbours. We were a motley assemblage of people, and we had a good many boys and young men among us; we had also many girls and young women. To represent, however, that we did not include a very great number, and a very fair proportion of family groups, would be to make a gross misstatement. Such groups were to be seen in all parts of the house; in the boxes and stalls particularly, they were composed of persons of very decent appearance, who had many children with them. Among our dresses there were most kinds of shabby and greasy wear, and much fustian and corduroy that was neither sound nor fragrant. The caps of our young men were mostly of a limp character, and we who wore them, slouched, high-shouldered, into our places with our hands in our pockets, and occasionally twisted our cravats about our necks like eels, and occasionally tied them down our breasts like links of sausages, and occasionally had a screw in our hair over each cheek-bone with a slight Thief-flavour in it. Besides prowlers and idlers, we were mechanics, dock-labourers, costermongers, petty tradesmen, small clerks, milliners, stay-makers, shoe-binders, slop workers, poor workers in a hundred highways and byeways. Many of us—on the whole, the majority—were not at all clean, and not at all choice in our lives or conversation. But we had all come together in a place where our convenience was well consulted, and where we were well looked after, to enjoy an evening's entertainment in common. We were not going to lose any part of what we had paid for, through anybody's caprice, and as a community we had a character to lose. So, we were closely attentive, and kept excellent order; and let the man or boy who did otherwise instantly get out from this place, or we would put him out with the greatest expedition.

We began at half-past six with a pantomime—with a

pantomime so long, that before it was over I felt as if I had been travelling for six weeks—going to India, say, by the Overland Mail. The Spirit of Liberty was the principal personage in the Introduction, and the Four Quarters of the World came out of the globe, glittering, and discoursed with the Spirit, who sang charmingly. We were delighted to understand that there was no Liberty anywhere but among ourselves, and we highly applauded the agreeable fact. In an allegorical way, which did as well as any other way, we and the Spirit of Liberty got into a kingdom of Needles and Pins, and found them at war with a potentate who called in to his aid their old arch-enemy Rust, and who would have got the better of them if the Spirit of Liberty had not in the nick of time transformed the leaders into Clown, Pantaloon, Harlequin, Columbine, Harlequina, and a whole family of Sprites, consisting of a remarkably stout father and three spineless sons. We all knew what was coming when the Spirit of Liberty addressed the king with the big face, and His Majesty backed to the side-scenes and began untying himself behind, with his big face all on one side. Our excitement at that crisis was great, and our delight unbounded. After this era in our existence, we went through all the incidents of a pantomime; it was not by any means a savage pantomime in the way of burning or boiling people, or throwing them out of window, or cutting them up; was often very droll; was always liberally got up, and cleverly presented. I noticed that the people who kept the shops, and who represented the passengers in the thoroughfares, and so forth, had no conventionality in them, but were unusually like the real thing—from which I infer that you may take that audience in (if you wish to) concerning Knights and Ladies, Fairies, Angels, or such like, but they are not to be done as to anything in the streets. I noticed, also, that when two young men, dressed in exact imitation of the eel-and-sausage-cravated portion of the audience, were chased by policemen, and, finding themselves in danger of being caught, dropped so suddenly as to oblige the policemen to tumble over them, there was great rejoicing among the caps—as though it were a delicate reference to something they had heard of before.

The Pantomime was succeeded by a Melo-Drama. Throughout the evening, I was pleased to observe Virtue quite as triumphant as she usually is out of doors, and indeed I thought rather more so. We all agreed (for the time) that honesty was the best policy, and we were as hard as iron upon Vice, and we wouldn't hear of Villany getting on in the world—no, not on any consideration whatever.

Between the pieces, we almost all of us went out and refreshed. Many of us went the length of drinking beer at the bar of the neighbouring public-house, some of us drank spirits, crowds of us had sandwiches and ginger-beer at the refreshment-bars established for us in the Theatre. The sandwich—as substantial as was consistent with portability, and as cheap as possible—we hailed as one of our greatest institutions. It forced its way among us at all stages of the entertainment, and we were always delighted to see it; its adaptability to the varying moods of our nature was surprising; we could never weep so comfortably as when our tears fell on our sandwich; we could never laugh so heartily as when we choked with sandwich; Virtue never looked so beautiful or Vice so deformed as when we paused, sandwich in hand, to consider what would come of that resolution of Wickedness in boots, to sever Innocence in flowered chintz from Honest Industry in striped stockings. When the curtain fell for the night, we still fell back upon sandwich, to help us through the rain and mire, and home to bed.

This, as I have mentioned, was Saturday night. Being Saturday night, I had accomplished but the half of my uncommercial journey; for, its object was to compare the play on Saturday evening, with the preaching in the same Theatre on Sunday evening.

Therefore, at the same hour of half-past six on the similarly damp and muddy Sunday evening, I returned to this Theatre. I drove up to the entrance (fearful of being late, or I should have come on foot), and found myself in a large crowd of people who, I am happy to state, were put into excellent spirits by my arrival. Having nothing to look at but the mud and the closed doors, they looked at me, and highly enjoyed the comic spectacle. My modesty inducing me to draw off, some hundreds of yards, into a dark corner, they at once forgot me, and applied themselves to their former occupation of looking at the mud and looking in at the closed doors: which, being of grated iron-work, allowed the lighted passage within to be seen. They were chiefly people of respectable appearance, odd and impulsive as most crowds are, and making a joke of being there as most crowds do.

In the dark corner I might have sat a long while, but that a very obliging passer-by informed me that the Theatre was already full, and that the people whom I saw in the street were all shut out for want of room. After that, I lost no time in worming myself into the building, and creeping to a place in a Proscenium box that had been kept for me.

There must have been full four thousand people present. Carefully estimating the pit alone, I could bring it out as holding little less than fourteen hundred. Every part of the house was well filled, and I had not found it easy to make my way along the back of the boxes to where I sat. The chandeliers in the ceiling were lighted; there was no light on the stage; the orchestra was empty. The green curtain was down, and, packed pretty closely on chairs on the small space of stage before it, were some thirty gentlemen, and two or three ladies. In the centre of these, in a desk or pulpit covered with red baize, was the presiding minister. The kind of rostrum he occupied, will be very well understood, if I liken it to a boarded-up-fireplace turned towards the audience, with a gentleman in a black surtout standing in the stove and leaning forward over the mantelpiece.

A portion of Scripture was being read when I went in. It was followed by a discourse, to which the congregation listened with most exemplary attention and uninterrupted silence and decorum. My own attention comprehended both the auditory and the speaker, and shall turn to both in this recalling of the scene, exactly as it did at the time.

"A very difficult thing," I thought, when the discourse began, "to speak appropriately to so large an audience, and to speak with tact. Without it, better not to speak at all. Infinitely better, to read the New Testament well, and to let *that* speak. In this congregation there is indubitably one pulse; but I doubt if any power short of genius can touch it as one, and make it answer as one."

I could not possibly say to myself as the discourse proceeded, that the minister was a good speaker. I could not possibly say to myself that he expressed an understanding of the general mind and character of his audience. There was a supposititious working-man introduced into the homily, to make supposititious objections to our Christian religion and be reasoned down, who was not only a very disagreeable person, but remarkably unlike life—very much more unlike it than anything I had seen in the pantomime. The native independence of character this artisan was supposed to possess, was represented by a suggestion of a dialect that I certainly never heard in my uncommercial travels, and with a coarse swing of voice and manner anything but agreeable to his feelings I should conceive, considered in the light of a portrait, and as far away from the fact as a Chinese Tartar. There was a model pauper introduced in like manner, who appeared to me to be the most intolerably arrogant pauper ever relieved, and to show himself in absolute want and dire necessity of a course of Stone Yard. For, how did this pauper testify to his having received the gospel of humility? A gentleman met him in the workhouse, and said (which I myself really thought good-natured of him), "Ah, John? I am sorry to see you here. I am sorry to see you so poor." "Poor, sir!" replied that man, drawing himself up, "I am the son of a Prince! *My* father is the King of Kings. *My* father is the Lord of Lords. *My* father is the ruler of all the Princes of the Earth!" &c. And this was what all the preacher's fellow-sinners might come to, if they would embrace this blessed book—which I must say it did some violence to my own feelings of reverence, to see held out at arm's length at frequent intervals and soundingly slapped, like a slow lot at a sale. Now, could I help asking myself the question, whether the mechanic before me, who must detect the preacher as being wrong about the visible manner of himself and the like of himself, and about such a noisy lip-server as that pauper, might not, most unhappily for the usefulness of the occasion, doubt that preacher's being right about things not visible to human senses?

Again. Is it necessary or advisable to address such an audience continually, as "fellow-sinners"? Is it not enough to be fellow-creatures, born yesterday, suffering and striving to-day, dying to-morrow? By our common humanity, my brothers and sisters, by our common capacities for pain and pleasure, by our common laughter and our common tears, by our common aspiration to reach something better than ourselves, by our common tendency to believe in something good, and to invest whatever we love or whatever we lose with some qualities that are superior to our own failings and weaknesses as we know them in our own poor hearts—by these. Hear me!—Surely, it is enough to be fellow-creatures. Surely, it includes the other designation and some touching meanings over and above.

Again. There was a personage introduced into the discourse (not an absolute novelty, to the best of my remembrance of my reading), who had been personally known to the preacher, and had been quite a Crichton in all the ways of philosophy, but had been an infidel. Many a time had the preacher talked with him on that subject, and many a time had he failed to convince that intelligent man. But he fell ill, and died, and before he died he recorded his conversion—in words which the preacher had taken down, my fellow-sinners, and would read to you from this piece of paper. I must confess that to me, as one of an uninstructed audience, they did not appear particularly edifying. I thought their tone extremely selfish, and I thought they had a spiritual vanity in them which was of the before-mentioned refractory pauper's family.

All slangs and twangs are objectionable everywhere, but the slang and twang of the conventicle—as bad in its way as that of the House of Commons, and nothing worse can be said of it—should be studiously avoided under such circumstances as I describe. The avoidance was not complete on this occasion. Nor was it quite agreeable to see the preacher addressing his pet " points" to his backers on the stage, as if appealing to those disciples to show him up, and testify to the multitude that each of those points was a clincher.

But, in respect of the large Christianity of his general tone; of his renunciation of all priestly authority; of his earnest and reiterated assurance to the people that the commonest among them could work out their own salvation if they would, by simply, lovingly, and dutifully following Our Saviour, and that they needed the mediation of no erring man; in these particulars, this gentleman deserved all praise. Nothing could be better than the spirit, or the plain emphatic words of his discourse in these respects. And it was a most significant and encouraging circumstance that whenever he struck that chord, or whenever he described anything which Christ himself had done, the array of faces before him was very much more earnest, and very much more expressive of emotion, than at any other time.

And now, I am brought to the fact, that the lowest part of the audience of the previous night, *was not there.* There is no doubt about it. There was no such thing in that building, that Sunday evening. I have been told since, that the lowest part of the audience of the Victoria Theatre has been attracted to its Sunday services. I have been very glad to hear it, but on this occasion of which I write, the lowest part of the usual audience of the Britannia Theatre, decidedly and unquestionably stayed away. When I first took my seat and looked at the house, my surprise at the change in its occupants was as great as my disappointment. To the most respectable class of the previous evening, was added a great number of respectable strangers attracted by curiosity, and drafts from the regular congregations of various chapels. It was impossible to fail in identifying the character of these last, and they were very numerous. I came out in a strong, slow tide of them setting from the boxes. Indeed, while the discourse was in progress, the respectable character of the auditory was so manifest in their appearance, that when the minister addressed a supposititious "outcast," one really felt a little impatient of it, as a figure of speech not justified by anything the eye could discover.

The time appointed for the conclusion of the proceedings was eight o'clock. The address having lasted until full that time, and it being the custom to conclude with a hymn, the preacher intimated in a few sensible words that the clock had struck the hour, and that those who desired to go before the hymn was sung, could go now, without giving offence. No one stirred. The hymn was then sung, in good time and tune and unison, and its effect was very striking. A comprehensive benevolent prayer dismissed the throng, and in seven or eight minutes there was nothing left in the Theatre but a light cloud of dust.

That these Sunday meetings in Theatres are good things, I do not doubt. Nor do I doubt that they will work lower and lower down in the social scale, if those who preside over them will be very careful on two heads: firstly, not to disparage the places in which they speak, or the intelligence of their hearers; secondly, not to set themselves in antagonism to the natural inborn desire of the mass of mankind to recreate themselves and to be amused.

There is a third head, taking precedence of all others, to which my remarks on the discourse I heard, have tended. In the New Testament there is the most beautiful and affecting history conceivable by man, and there are the terse models for all prayer and for all preaching. As to the models, imitate them, Sunday preachers—else why are they there, consider? As to the history, tell it. Some people cannot read, some people will not read, many people (this especially holds among the young and ignorant) find it hard to pursue the verse-form in which the book is presented to them, and imagine that those breaks imply gaps, and want of continuity. Help them over that first stumbling-block, by setting forth the history in narrative, with no fear of exhausting it. You will never preach so well, you will never move them so profoundly, you will never send them away with half so much to think of. Which is the better interest: Christ's choice of twelve poor men to help in those merciful wonders among the poor and rejected; or the pious bullying of a whole Union-full of paupers? What is your changed philosopher to wretched me, peeping in at the door out of the mud of the streets and of my life, when you have the widow's son to tell me about, the ruler's daughter, the other figure at the door when the brother of the two sisters was dead, and one of the two ran to the mourner, crying, "The Master is come and calleth for thee"?—Let the preacher who will thoroughly forget himself and remember no individuality but one, and no eloquence but one, stand up before four thousand men and women at the Britannia Theatre any Sunday night, recounting that narrative to them as fellow-creatures, and he shall see a sight!

V.

POOR MERCANTILE JACK.

Is the sweet little cherub who sits smiling aloft and keeps watch on the life of poor Jack, commissioned to take charge of Mercantile Jack, as well as Jack of the national navy? If not, who is? What is the cherub about, and what are we all about, when poor Mercantile Jack is having his brains slowly knocked out by pennyweights, aboard the brig Beelzebub, or the barque Bowie-knife—when he looks his last at that infernal craft, with the first officer's iron boot-heel in his remaining eye, or with his dying body towed overboard in the ship's wake, while the cruel wounds in it do "the multitudinous seas incarnadine"?

Is it unreasonable to entertain a belief that if, aboard the brig Beelzebub or the barque Bowie-knife, the first officer did half the damage to cotton that he does to men, there would presently arise from both sides of the Atlantic so vociferous an invocation of the sweet little cherub who sits calculating aloft, keeping watch on the markets that pay, that such vigilant cherub would, with a winged sword, have that gallant officer's organ of destructiveness out of his head in the space of a flash of lightning?

If it be unreasonable, then am I the most unreasonable of men, for I believe it with all my soul.

This was my thought as I walked the dock-quays at Liverpool, keeping watch on poor Mercantile Jack. Alas for me! I have long outgrown the state of sweet little cherub; but there I was, and there Mercantile Jack was, and very busy he was, and very cold he was: the snow yet lying in the frozen furrows of the land, and the north-east winds snipping off the tops of the little waves in the Mersey, and rolling them into hailstones to pelt him with. Mercantile Jack was hard at it, in the hard weather: as he mostly is in all weathers, poor Jack. He was girded to ships' masts and funnels of steamers, like a forester to a great oak, scraping and painting; he was lying out on yards, furling sails that tried to beat him off; he was dimly discernible up in a world of giant cobwebs, reefing and splicing; he was faintly audible down in holds, stowing and unshipping cargo; he was winding round and round at capstans melodious, monotonous, and drunk; he was of a diabolical aspect, with coaling for the Antipodes; he was washing decks barefoot, with the breast of his red shirt open to the blast, though it was sharper than the knife in his leathern girdle; he was looking over bulwarks, all eyes and hair; he was standing by at the shoot of the Cunard steamer, off to-morrow, as the stocks in trade of several butchers, poulterers, and fishmongers, poured down into the ice-house; he was coming aboard of other vessels, with his kit in a tarpaulin bag, attended by plunderers to the very last moment of his shore-going existence. As though his senses when released from the uproar of the elements, were under obligation to be confused by other turmoil, there was a rattling of wheels, a clattering of hoofs, a clashing of iron, a jolting of cotton and hides and casks and timber, an incessant deafening disturbance, on the quays, that was the very madness of sound. And as, in the midst of it, he stood swaying about, with his hair blown all manner of wild ways, rather crazedly taking leave of his plunderers, all the rigging in the docks was shrill in the wind, and every little steamer coming and going across the Mersey was sharp in its blowing off, and every buoy in the river bobbed spitefully up and down, as if there were a general taunting chorus of "Come along, Mercantile Jack! Ill-lodged, ill-fed, ill-used, hocussed, entrapped, anticipated, cleaned out. Come along, Poor Mercantile Jack, and be tempest-tossed till you are drowned!"

The uncommercial transaction which had brought me and Jack together, was this;—I had entered the Liverpool police-force, that I might have a look at the various unlawful traps which are every night set for Jack. As my term of service in that distinguished corps was short, and as my personal bias in the capacity of one of its members has ceased, no suspicion will attach to my evidence that it is an admirable force. Besides that it is composed, without favour, of the best men that can be picked, it is directed by an unusual intelligence. Its organisation against Fires, I take to be much better than the metropolitan system, and in all respects it tempers its remarkable vigilance with a still more remarkable discretion.

Jack had knocked off work in the docks some hours, and I had taken, for purposes of identification, a photograph-likeness of a thief, in the portrait-room at our head police office (on the whole, he seemed rather complimented by the proceeding), and I had been on police-parade, and the small hand of the clock was moving on to ten, when I took up my lantern to follow Mr. Superintendent to the traps that were set for Jack. In Mr. Superintendent I saw, as anybody might, a tall well-looking well set-up man of a soldierly bearing, with a cavalry air, a good chest, and a resolute but not by any means ungentle face. He carried in his hand a plain black walking-stick of hard wood; and whenever and wherever, at any after-time of the night, he struck it on the pavement with a ringing sound, it instantly produced a whistle out of the darkness, and a policeman. To this remarkable stick, I refer an air of mystery and magic which pervaded the whole of my perquisition among the traps that were set for Jack.

We began by diving into the obscurest streets and lanes of the port. Suddenly pausing in a flow of cheerful discourse, before a dead wall, apparently some ten miles long, Mr. Superintendent struck upon the ground, and the wall opened and shot out, with military salute of hand to temple, two policemen—not in the least surprised themselves, not in the least surprising Mr. Superintendent.

"All right, Sharpeye?"

"All right, sir."

"All right, Trampfoot?"

"All right, sir."

"Is Quickear there?"

"Here am I, sir."

"Come with us."

"Yes, sir."

So, Sharpeye went before, and Mr. Superintendent and I went next, and Trampfoot and Quickear marched as rear-guard. Sharpeye, I soon had occasion to remark, had a skilful and quite professional way of opening doors—touched latches delicately, as if they were keys of musical instruments—opened every door he touched, as if he were perfectly confident that there was stolen property behind it—instantly insinuated himself, to prevent its being shut.

Sharpeye opened several doors of traps that were set for Jack, but Jack did not happen to be in any of them. They were all such miserable places that really, Jack, if I were you, I would give them a wider berth. In every trap, somebody was sitting over a fire, waiting for Jack. Now, it was a crouching old woman, like the picture of the Norwood Gipsy in the old sixpenny dream-books; now, it was a crimp of the male sex in a checked shirt and without a coat, reading a newspaper; now, it was a man crimp and a woman crimp, who always introduced themselves as united in holy matrimony; now, it was Jack's delight, his (un) lovely Nan; but they were all waiting for Jack, and were all frightfully disappointed to see us.

"Who have you got up-stairs here?" says Sharpeye, generally. (In the Move-on tone.)

"Nobody, surr; sure not a blessed sowl!" (Irish feminine reply.)

"What do you mean by nobody? Didn't I hear a woman's step go up-stairs when my hand was on the latch?"

"Ah! sure thin you're right, surr, I forgot her! 'Tis on'y Betsy White, surr. Ah! you know Betsy, surr. Come down, Betsy darlin', and say the gintlemin."

Generally, Betsy looks over the banisters (the steep staircase is in the room) with a forcible expression in her protesting face, of an intention to compensate herself for the present trial by grinding Jack finer than usual when he does come. Generally, Sharpeye turns to Mr. Superintendent, and says, as if the subjects of his remarks were wax-work:

"One of the worst, sir, this house is. This woman has been indicted three times. This man's a regular bad one likewise. His real name is Pegg. Gives himself out as Waterhouse."

"Never had sitch a name as Pegg near me back, thin, since I was in this house, bee the good Lard!" says the woman.

Generally, the man says nothing at all, but becomes exceedingly round-shouldered, and pretends to read his paper with rapt attention. Generally, Sharpeye directs our observation with a look, to the prints and pictures that are invariably numerous on the walls. Always, Trampfoot and Quickear are taking notice on the doorstep. In default of Sharpeye being acquainted with the exact individuality of any gentleman encountered, one of these two is sure to proclaim from the outer air, like a gruff spectre, that Jackson is not Jackson, but knows himself to be Fogle; or that Canlon is Walker's brother, against whom there was not sufficient evidence; or that the man who says he never was at sea since he was a boy, came ashore from a voyage last Thursday, or sails tomorrow morning. "And that is a bad class of man, you see," says Mr. Superintendent, when he got out into the dark again, "and very difficult to deal with, who, when he has made this place too hot to hold him, enters himself for a voyage as steward or cook, and is out of knowledge for months, and then turns up again worse than ever."

When we had gone into many such houses, and had come out (always leaving everybody relapsing into waiting for Jack), we started off to a singing-house where Jack was expected to muster strong.

The vocalisation was taking place in a long low room up-stairs; at one end, an orchestra of two performers, and a small platform; across the room, a series of open pews for Jack, with an aisle down the middle; at the other end, a larger pew than the rest, entitled SNUG, and reserved for mates and similar good company. About the room, some amazing coffee-coloured pictures varnished an inch deep, and some stuffed creatures in cases; dotted among the audience, in Snug and out of Snug, the "Professionals;" among them, the celebrated comic favourite Mr. Banjo Bones, looking very hideous with his blackened face and limp sugar-loaf hat; beside him, sipping rum-and-water, Mrs. Banjo Bones, in her natural colours—a little heightened.

It was a Friday night, and Friday night was considered not a good night for Jack. At any rate, Jack did not show in very great force even here, though the house was one to which he much resorts, and where a good deal of money is taken. There was British Jack, a little maudlin and sleepy, lolling over his empty glass, as if he were trying to read his fortune at the bottom; there was Loafing Jack of the Stars and Stripes, rather an unpromising customer, with his long nose, lank cheek, high cheek-bones, and nothing soft about him but his cabbage-leaf hat; there was Spanish Jack with curls of black hair, rings in his ears, and a knife not far from his hand, if you got into trouble with him; there were Maltese Jack, and Jack of Sweden, and Jack the Finn, looming through the smoke of their pipes, and turning faces that looked as if they were carved out of dark wood, towards the young lady dancing the hornpipe: who found the platform so exceedingly small for it, that I had a nervous expectation of seeing her, in the backward steps, disappear through the window. Still, if all hands had been got together, they would not have more than half filled the room. Observe, however, said Mr. Licensed Victualler, the host, that it was Friday night, and, besides, it was getting on for twelve, and Jack had gone aboard. A sharp and watchful man, Mr. Licensed Victualler, the host, with tight lips and a complete edition of Cocker's arithmetic in each eye. Attended to his business himself, he said. Always on the spot. When he heard of talent, trusted nobody's account of it, but went off by rail to see it. If true talent, engaged it. Pounds a week for talent—four pound—five pound. Banjo Bones was undoubted talent. Hear this instrument that was going to play—it was real talent! In truth it was very good; a kind of piano-accordion, played by a young girl of a delicate prettiness of face, figure, and dress, that made the audience look coarser. She sang to the instrument, too; first, a song about village bells, and how they chimed; then a song about how I went to sea; winding up with an imitation of the bagpipes, which Mercantile Jack seemed to understand much the best. A good girl, said Mr. Licensed Victualler. Kept herself select. Sat in Snug, not listening to the blandishments of Mates. Lived with mother. Father dead. Once a merchant well to do, but over speculated himself. On delicate inquiry as to salary paid for item of talent under consideration, Mr. Victualler's pounds dropped suddenly to shillings—still it was a very comfortable thing for a young person like that, you know; she only went on six times a night, and was only required to be there from six at night to twelve. What was more conclusive was, Mr. Victualler's assurance that he "never allowed any language, and never suffered any disturbance." Sharpeye confirmed the

F

statement, and the order that prevailed was the best proof of it that could have been cited. So, I came to the conclusion that poor Mercantile Jack might do (as I am afraid he does) much worse than trust himself to Mr. Victualler, and pass his evenings here.

But we had not yet looked, Mr. Superintendent—said Trampfoot, receiving us in the street again with military salute—for Dark Jack. True, Trampfoot. Ring the wonderful stick, rub the wonderful lantern, and cause the spirits of the stick and lantern to convey us to the Darkies.

There was no disappointment in the matter of Dark Jack; *he* was producible. The Genii set us down in the little first floor of a little public-house, and there, in a stiflingly close atmosphere, were Dark Jack and Dark Jack's Delight, his *white* unlovely Nan, sitting against the wall all round the room. More than that: Dark Jack's Delight was the least unlovely Nan, both morally and physically, that I saw that night.

As a fiddle and tambourine band were sitting among the company, Quickear suggested why not strike up? "Ah la'ads!" said a negro sitting by the door, "gib the jebblem a darnse. Tak' yah pardlers, jebblem, for 'um QUAD-rill."

This was the landlord, in a Greek cap, and a dress half Greek and half English. As master of the ceremonies, he called all the figures, and occasionally addressed himself parenthetically—after this manner. When he was very loud, I use capitals.

"Now den! Hoy! ONE. Right and left. (Put a

steam on, gib 'um powder.) LA-dies' chail. BAL-loon say. Lemonade! Two. AD-warnse and go back (gib 'ell a breakdown, shake it out o' yerselbs, keep a movil). SWING-corners, BAL-loon say, and Lemonade! (Hoy!) THREE. GENT come for'ard with a lady and go back, hoppersite come for'ard and do what yer can. (Aeiohoy!) BAL-loon say, and leetle lemonade (Dat hair nigger by 'um fireplace 'hind a' time, shake it out o' yerselbs, gib 'ell a breakdown). Now den! Hoy! FOUR! Lemonade. BAL-loon say, and swing. FOUR ladies meets in 'um middle, FOUR gents goes round 'um ladies, FOUR gents passes out under 'um ladies' arms, SWING—and Lemonade till 'a moosic can't play no more! (Hoy, Hoy!)"

The male dancers were all blacks, and one was an unusually powerful man of six feet three or four. The sound of their flat feet on the floor was as unlike the sound of white feet as their faces were unlike white faces. They toed and heeled, shuffled, double-shuffled, double-double-shuffled, covered the buckle, and beat the time out, rarely, dancing with a great show of teeth, and with a childish good-humoured enjoyment that was very prepossessing. They generally kept together, these poor fellows, said Mr. Superintendent, because they were at a disadvantage singly, and liable to slights in the neighbouring streets. But, if I were Light Jack, I should be very slow to interfere oppressively with Dark Jack, for, whenever I have had to do with him I have found him a simple and a gentle fellow. Bearing this in mind, I asked his friendly permission to leave him restoration of beer, in wishing him good night, and thus it fell out that the last words I heard him say as I blundered down the worn stairs, were, "Jcbblem's elth! Ladies drinks fust!"

The night was now well on into the morning, but, for miles and hours we explored a strange world, where nobody ever goes to bed, but everybody is eternally sitting up, waiting for Jack. This exploration was among a labyrinth of dismal courts and blind alleys, called Entries, kept in wonderful order by the police, and in much better order than by the corporation: the want of gaslight in the most dangerous and infamous of these places being quite unworthy of so spirited a town. I need describe but two or three of the houses in which Jack was waited for as specimens of the rest. Many we attained by noisome passages so profoundly dark that we felt our way with our hands. Not one of the whole number we visited, was without its show of prints and ornamental crockery; the quantity of the latter set forth on little shelves and in little cases, in otherwise wretched rooms, indicating that Mercantile Jack must have an extraordinary fondness for crockery, to necessitate so much of that bait in his traps.

Among such garniture, in one front parlour in the dead of the night, four women were sitting by a fire. One of them had a male child in her arms. On a stool among them was a swarthy youth with a guitar, who had evidently stopped playing when our footsteps were heard.

"Well! how do *you* do?" says Mr. Superintendent, looking about him.

"Pretty well, sir, and hope you gentlemen are going to treat us ladies, now you have come to see us."

"Order there!" says Sharpeye.

"None of that!" says Quickear.

Trampfoot, outside, is heard to confide to himself, "Meggisson's lot this is. And a bad 'un!"

"Well!" says Mr. Superintendent, laying his hand on the shoulder of the swarthy youth, "and who's this?"

"Antonio, sir."

"And what does *he* do here?"

"Come to give us a bit of music. No harm in that, I suppose?"

"A young foreign sailor?"

"Yes. He's a Spaniard. You're a Spaniard, ain't you, Antonio?"

"Me Spanish."

"And he don't know a word you say, not he, not if you was to talk to him till doomsday." (Triumphantly, as if it redounded to the credit of the house.)

"Will he play something?"

"Oh, yes, if you like. Play something, Antonio. *You* ain't ashamed to play something; are you?"

The cracked guitar raises the feeblest ghost of a tune, and three of the women keep time to it with their heads, and the fourth with the child. If Antonio has brought any money in with him, I am afraid he will never take it out, and it even strikes me that his jacket and guitar may be in a bad way. But, the look of the young man and the tinkling of the instrument so change the place in a moment to a leaf out of Don Quixote, that I wonder where his mule is stabled, until he leaves off.

I am bound to acknowledge (as it tends rather to my uncommercial confusion), that I occasioned a difficulty in this establishment, by having taken the child in my arms. For, on my offering to restore it to a ferocious joker not unstimulated by rum, who claimed to be its mother, that unnatural parent put her hands behind her, and declined to accept it; backing into the fireplace, and very shrilly declaring, regardless of remonstrance from her friends, that she knowed it to be Law, that whoever took a child from its mother of his own will, was bound to stick to it. The uncommercial sense of being in a rather ridiculous position with the poor little child beginning to be frightened, was relieved by my worthy friend and fellow-constable, Trampfoot; who, laying hands on the article as if it were a Bottle, passed it on to the nearest woman, and bade her "take hold of that." As we came out, the Bottle was passed to the ferocious joker, and they all sat down as before, including Antonio and the guitar. It was clear that there was no such thing as a nightcap to this baby's head, and that even he never went to bed, but was always kept up—and would grow up, kept up—waiting for Jack.

Later still in the night, we came (by the court "where the man was murdered," and by the other court across the street, into which his body was dragged) to another parlour in another Entry, where several people were sitting round a fire in just the same way. It was a dirty and offensive place, with some ragged clothes drying in it; but there was a high shelf over the entrance-door (to be out of the reach of marauding hands, possibly) with two large white loaves on it, and a great piece of Cheshire cheese.

"Well!" says Mr. Superintendent, with a comprehensive look all round. "How do *you* do?"

"Not much to boast of, sir." From the curtseying woman of the house. "This is my good man, sir."

"You are not registered as a common Lodging House?"

"No, sir."

Sharpeye (in the Move-on tone) puts in the pertinent inquiry, "Then why ain't you?"

"Ain't got no one here, Mr. Sharpeye," rejoins the woman and my good man together, "but our own family."

"How many are you in family?"

The woman takes time to count, under pretence of coughing, and adds, as one scant of breath, "Seven, sir."

But she has missed one, so Sharpeye, who knows all about it, says:

"Here's a young man here makes eight, who ain't of your family?"

"No, Mr. Sharpeye, he's a weekly lodger."

"What does he do for a living?"

The young man here, takes the reply upon himself, and shortly answers, "Ain't got nothing to do."

The young man here, is modestly brooding behind a damp apron pendent from a clothes-line. As I glance at him I become—but I don't know why—vaguely reminded of Woolwich, Chatham, Portsmouth, and Dover. When we get out, my respected fellow-constable Sharpeye addressing Mr. Superintendent, says:

"You noticed that young man, sir, in at Darby's?"

"Yes. What is he?"

"Deserter, sir."

Mr. Sharpeye further intimates that when we have done with his services, he will step back and take that young man. Which in course of time he does: feeling at perfect ease about finding him, and knowing for a moral certainty that nobody in that region will be gone to bed.

Later still in the night, we came to another parlour up a step or two from the street, which was very cleanly, neatly, even tastefully, kept, and in which, set forth on a draped chest of drawers masking the staircase, was such a profusion of ornamental crockery, that it would have furnished forth a handsome sale-booth at a fair. It backed up a stout old lady—HOGARTH drew her exact likeness more than once—and a boy who was carefully writing a copy in a copy-book.

"Well, ma'am, how do *you* do?"

Sweetly, she can assure the dear gentlemen, sweetly. Charmingly, charmingly. And overjoyed to see us!

"Why, this is a strange time for this boy to be writing his copy. In the middle of the night!"

"So it is, dear gentlemen, Heaven bless your welcome faces and send ye prosperous, but he has been to the Play with a young friend for his diversion, and he combinates his improvement with entertainment, by doing his school-writhing afterwards, God be good to ye!"

The copy admonished human nature, to subjugate the fire of every fierce desire. One might have thought it recommended stirring the fire, the old lady so approved it. There she sat, rosily beaming at the copy-book and the boy, and invoking showers of blessings on our heads, when we left her in the middle of the night, waiting for Jack.

Later still in the night, we came to a nauseous room with an earth floor, into which the refuse scum of an alley trickled. The stench of this habitation was abominable; the seeming poverty of it, diseased and dire. Yet, here again, was visitor or lodger—a man sitting before the fire, like the rest of them elsewhere, and apparently not distasteful to the mistress's niece, who was also before the fire. The mistress herself had the misfortune of being in jail.

Three weird old women of transcendent ghastliness, were at needlework at a table in this room. Says Trampfoot to First Witch, "What are you making?" Says she, "Money-bags."

"*What* are you making?" retorts Trampfoot, a little off his balance.

"Bags to hold your money," says the witch, shaking her head, and setting her teeth; "you as has got it."

She holds up a common cash-bag, and on the table is a heap of such bags. Witch Two laughs at us. Witch Three scowls at us. Witch sisterhood all, stitch, stitch.

First Witch has a red circle round each eye. I fancy it like the beginning of the development of a perverted diabolical halo, and that when it spreads all round her head, she will die in the odour of devilry.

Trampfoot wishes to be informed what First Witch has got behind the table, down by the side of her, there? Witches Two and Three croak angrily, " Show him the child!"

She drags out a skinny little arm from a brown dust-heap on the ground. Adjured not to disturb the child, she lets it drop again. Thus we find at last that there is one child in the world of Entries who goes to bed—if this be bed.

Mr. Superintendent asks how long are they going to work at those bags?

How long? First Witch repeats. Going to have supper presently. See the cups and saucers, and the plates.

"Late? Ay! But we has to 'arn our supper afore we eats it!" Both the other witches repeat this after First Witch, and take the Uncommercial measurement with their eyes, as for a charmed winding-sheet. Some grim discourse ensues, referring to the mistress of the cave, who will be released from jail to-morrow. Witches pronounce Trampfoot "right there," when he deems it a trying distance for the old lady to walk; she shall be fetched by niece in a spring-cart.

As I took a parting look at First Witch in turning away, the red marks round her eyes seemed to have already grown larger, and she hungrily and thirstily looked out beyond me into the dark doorway, to see if Jack were there. For, Jack came even here, and the mistress had got into jail through deluding Jack.

When I at last ended this night of travel and got to bed, I failed to keep my mind on comfortable thoughts of Seaman's Homes (not overdone with strictness), and improved dock regulations giving Jack greater benefit of fire and candle aboard ship, through my mind's wandering among the vermin I had seen. Afterwards the same vermin ran all over my sleep. Evermore, when on a breezy day I see Poor Mercantile Jack running into port with a fair wind under all sail, I shall think of the unsleeping host of devourers who never go to bed, and are always in their set traps waiting for him.

VI.

REFRESHMENTS FOR TRAVELLERS.

In the late high winds I was blown to a great many places—and indeed, wind or no wind, I generally have extensive transactions on hand in the article of Air—but I have not been blown to any English place lately, and I very seldom have blown to any English place in my life, where I could get anything good to eat and drink in five minutes, or where, if I sought it, I was received with a welcome.

This is a curious thing to consider. But before (stimulated by my own experiences and the representations of many fellow-travellers of every uncommercial and commercial degree) I consider it further, I must utter a passing word of wonder concerning high winds.

I wonder why metropolitan gales always blow so hard at Walworth. I cannot imagine what Walworth has done, to bring such windy punishment upon itself, as I never fail to find recorded in the newspapers when the wind has blown at all hard. Brixton seems to have something on its conscience; Peckham suffers more than a virtuous Peckham might be supposed to deserve; the howling neighbourhood of Deptford figures largely in the accounts of the ingenious gentlemen who are out in every wind that blows, and to whom it is an ill high wind that blows no good; but, there can hardly be any Walworth left by this time. It must surely be blown away. I have read of more chimney-stacks and house-copings coming down with terrific smashes at Walworth, and of more sacred edifices being nearly (not quite) blown out to sea from the same accursed locality, than I have read of practised thieves with the appearance and manners of gentlemen—a popular phenomenon which never existed on earth out of fiction and a police report. Again: I wonder why people are always blown into the Surrey Canal, and into no other piece of water? Why do people get up early and go out in groups, to be blown into the Surrey Canal? Do they say to one another, "Welcome Death, so that we get into the newspapers"? Even that would be an insufficient explanation, because even then they might sometimes put themselves in the way of being blown into the Regent's Canal, instead of always saddling Surrey for the field. Some nameless policeman, too, is constantly on the slightest provocation, getting himself blown into this same Surrey Canal. Will SIR RICHARD MAYNE see to it, and restrain that weak-minded and feeble-bodied constable?

To resume the consideration of the curious question of Refreshment. I am a Briton, and, as such, I am aware that I never will be a slave—and yet I have latent suspicion that there must be some slavery of wrong custom in this matter.

I travel by railroad. I start from home at seven or eight in the morning, after breakfasting hurriedly. What with skimming over the open landscape, what with mining in the damp bowels of the earth, what with banging booming and shrieking the scores of miles away, I am hungry when I arrive at the "Refreshment" station where I am expected. Please to observe, expected. I have said, I am hungry; perhaps I might say, with greater point and force, that I am to some extent exhausted, and that I need—in the expressive French sense of the word—to be restored. What is provided for my restoration? The apartment that is to restore me is a wind-trap, cunningly set to inveigle all the draughts in that country-side, and to communicate a special intensity and velocity to them as they rotate in two hurricanes: one, about my wretched head: one, about my wretched legs. The training of the young ladies behind the counter who are to restore me, has been from their infancy directed to the assumption of a defiant dramatic show that I am *not* expected. It is in vain for me to represent to them by my humble and conciliatory manners, that I wish to be liberal. It is in vain for me to represent to myself, for the encouragement of my sinking soul, that the young ladies have a pecuniary interest in my arrival. Neither my reason nor my feelings can make head against the cold glazed glare of eye with which I am assured that I am not expected, and not wanted. The solitary man among the bottles would sometimes take pity on me, if he dared, but he is powerless against the rights and mights of Woman. (Of the page I make no account, for, he is a boy, and therefore the natural enemy of Creation.) Chilling fast, in the deadly tornadoes to which my upper and lower extremities are exposed, and subdued by the moral disadvantage at which I stand, I turn my disconsolate eyes on the refreshments that are to restore me. I find that I must either scald my throat by insanely ladling into it, against time and for no wager, brown hot water stiffened with flour; or, I must make myself flaky and sick with Banbury cake; or, I must stuff into my delicate organisation, a currant pincushion which I know will swell into immeasurable dimensions when it has got there; or, I must extort from an iron-bound quarry, with a fork, as if I were farming an inhospitable soil, some glutinous lumps of gristle and grease, called pork-pie. While thus forlornly occupied, I find that the depressing banquet on the table is, in every phase of its profoundly unsatisfactory character, so like the banquet at the meanest and shabbiest of evening parties, that I begin to think I must have "brought down" to supper, the old lady unknown, blue with cold, who is setting her teeth on edge with a cool orange, at my elbow—that the pastrycook who has compounded for the company on the lowest terms per head, is a fraudulent bankrupt, redeeming his contract with the stale stock from his window—that, for some unexplained reason, the family giving the party have become my mortal foes, and have given it on purpose to affront me. Or, I fancy that I am "breaking up" again, at the evening conversazione at school, charged two-and-sixpence in the half-year's bill; or breaking down again at that celebrated evening party given at Mrs. Bogles's boarding-house when I was a boarder there, on which occasion Mrs. Bogles was taken in execution by a branch of the legal profession who got in as the harp, and was removed (with the keys and subscribed capital) to a place of durance, half an hour prior to the commencement of the festivities.

Take another case.

Mr. Grazinglands, of the Midland Counties, came to London by railroad one morning last week, accompanied by the amiable and fascinating Mrs. Grazinglands. Mr. G. is a gentleman of a comfortable property, and had a little business to transact at the Bank of England, which required the concurrence and signature of Mrs. G. Their business disposed of, Mr. and Mrs. Grazinglands viewed the Royal Exchange, and the exterior of St. Paul's Cathedral. The spirits of Mrs. Grazinglands then gradually beginning to flag, Mr. Grazinglands (who is the tenderest of husbands) remarked with sympathy, "Arabella, my dear, I fear you are faint." Mrs. Grazinglands replied, "Alexander, I am rather faint; but don't mind me, I shall be better presently." Touched by the feminine meekness of this answer, Mr. Grazinglands looked in at a pastrycook's window, hesitating as to the expediency of lunching at that establishment. He beheld nothing to eat, but butter in various forms, slightly charged with jam, and languidly frizzling over tepid water. Two ancient turtle-shells, on which was inscribed the legend, "Soups," decorated a glass partition within, enclosing a stuffy alcove, from which a ghastly mockery of a marriage-breakfast spread on a rickety table, warned the terrified traveller. An oblong box of stale and broken pastry at reduced prices, mounted on a stool, ornamented the doorway; and two high chairs that looked as if they were performing on stilts, embellished the counter. Over the whole, a young lady presided, whose gloomy haughtiness as she surveyed the street, announced a deep-seated grievance against society, and an implacable determination to be avenged. From a beetle-haunted kitchen below this institution, fumes arose, suggestive of a class of soup which Mr. Grazinglands knew, from painful experience, enfeebles the mind, distends the stomach, forces itself into the complexion, and tries to ooze out at the eyes. As he decided against entering, and turned away, Mrs. Grazinglands, becoming perceptibly weaker, repeated, " I am rather faint, Alexander, but don't mind me." Urged to new efforts by these words of resignation, Mr. Grazinglands looked in at a cold and floury baker's shop, where utilitarain buns unrelieved by a currant, consorted with hard biscuits, a stone filter of cold water, a hard pale clock, and a hard little old woman with flaxen hair, of an undeveloped-farinaceous aspect, as if she had been fed upon seeds. He might have entered even here, but for the timely remembrance coming upon him that Jairing's was but round the corner.

Now, Jairing's being an hotel for families and gentlemen, in high repute among the midland counties, Mr. Grazinglands plucked up a great spirit when he told Mrs. Grazinglands she should have a chop there. That lady, likewise, felt that she was going to see Life. Arriving on that gay and festive scene, they found the second waiter, in a flabby undress, cleaning the windows of the empty coffee-room; and the first waiter, denuded of his white tie, making up his cruets behind the Post-office Directory. The latter (who took them in hand) was greatly put out by their patronage, and showed his mind to be troubled by a sense of the pressing necessity of instantly smuggling Mrs. Grazinglands into the obscurest corner of the building. This slighted lady (who is the pride of her division of the county) was immediately conveyed, by several dark passages, and up and down several steps, into a penitential apartment at the back of the house, where five invalided old plate-warmers leaned up against one another under a discarded old melancholy sideboard, and where the wintry leaves of all the dining-tables in the house lay thick. Also, a sofa, of incomprehensible form regarded from any sofane point of view, murmured "Bed;" while an air of mingled fluffiness and heeltaps, added, "Second Waiter's." Secreted in this dismal hold, objects of a mysterious distrust and suspicion, Mr. Grazinglands and his charming partner waited twenty minutes for the smoke (for it never came to a fire), twenty-five minutes for the sherry, half an hour for the tablecloth, forty minutes for the knives and forks, three-quarters of an hour for the chops, and an hour for the potatoes. On settling the little bill—which was not much more than the day's pay of a Lieutenant in the navy—Mr. Grazinglands took heart to remonstrate against the general quality and cost of his reception. To whom the waiter replied, substantially, that Jairing's made it a merit to have accepted him on any terms; " for," added the waiter (unmistakably coughing at Mrs. Grazinglands, the pride of her division of the county), "when indiwiduals is not staying in the 'Ouse, their favours is not as a rule looked upon as making it worth Mr. Jairing's while; nor is it, indeed, a style of business Mr. Jairing wishes." Finally, Mr. and Mrs. Grazinglands passed out of Jairing's hotel for Families and Gentlemen, in a state of the greatest depression, scorned by the bar; and did not recover their self-respect for several days.

Or, take another case. Take your own case.

You are going off by railway, from any Terminus. You have twenty minutes for dinner, before you go. You want your dinner, and, like Doctor Johnson, Sir, you like to dine. You present to your mind, a picture of the refreshment-table at that terminus. The conventional shabby evening party supper—accepted as the model for all termini and all refreshment stations, because it is the last repast known to this state of existence of which any human creature would partake, but in the direst extremity—sickens your contemplation, and your words are these: "I cannot dine on stale sponge-cakes that turn to sand in the mouth. I cannot dine on shining brown patties, composed of unknown animals within, and offering to my view the device of an indigestible star-fish in leaden pie-crust without. I cannot dine on a sandwich that has long been pining under an exhausted receiver. I cannot dine on barley-sugar. I cannot dine on Toffee." You repair to the nearest hotel, and arrive, agitated, in the coffee-room.

It is a most astonishing fact that the waiter is very cold to you. Account for it how you may, smooth it over how you will, you cannot deny that he is cold to you. He is not glad to see you, he does not want you, he would much rather you hadn't come. He opposes to your flushed condition, an immovable composure. As if this were not enough, another waiter, born, as it would seem, expressly to look at you in this passage of your life, stands at a little distance, with his napkin under his arm and his hands folded, looking at you with all his might. You impress on your waiter that you have ten minutes for dinner, and he proposes that you shall begin with a bit of fish which will be ready in twenty. That proposal declined, he suggests—as a neat originality—" a weal or mutton cutlet." You close with either cutlet, any cutlet, any thing. He goes, leisurely, behind a door and calls down some unseen shaft. A* ventriloquial dialogue ensues, tending finally to the effect that weal only, is available on the spur of the moment. You anxiously call out, "Veal, then!" Your waiter, having settled that point, returns to array your tablecloth, with a table napkin folded cocked-hat wise (slowly, for something out of window engages his eye), a white wine-glass, a green wine-glass, a blue finger-glass, a tumbler, and a powerful field battery of fourteen castors with nothing in them; or at all events—which is enough for your purpose—with nothing in them that will come out. All this time, the other waiter looks at you—with an air of mental comparison and curiosity, now, as if it had occurred to him that you are rather like his brother. Half your time gone, and nothing come but the jug of ale and the bread, you implore your waiter to "see after that cutlet, waiter; pray do!" He cannot go at once, for he is carrying in seventeen pounds of American cheese for you to finish with, and a small Landed Estate of celery and watercresses. The other waiter changes his leg, and takes a new view of you—doubtfully, now, as if he had rejected the resemblance to his brother, and had begun to think you more like his aunt or his grandmother. Again you beseech your waiter with pathetic indignation, to "see after that cutlet!" He steps out to see after it, and by-and-by, when you are going away without it, comes back with it. Even then, he will not take the sham silver-cover off, without a pause for a flourish, and a look at the musty cutlet as if he were surprised to see it—which cannot possibly be the case, he must have seen it so often before. A sort of fur has been produced upon its surface by the cook's art, and, in a sham silver vessel staggering on two feet instead of three, is a cutaneous kind of sauce, of brown pimples and pickled cucumber. You order the bill, but your waiter cannot bring your bill yet, because he is bringing, instead, three flinty-hearted potatoes and two grim head of broccoli, like the occasional ornaments on area railings, badly boiled. You know that you will never come to this pass, any more than to the cheese and celery, and you imperatively demand your bill; but, it takes time to get, even when gone for, because your waiter has to communicate with a lady who lives behind a sash-window in a corner, and who appears to have to refer to several Ledgers before she can make it out—as if you had been staying there a year. You become distracted to get away, and the other waiter, once more changing his leg, still looks at you—but suspiciously, now, as if you had begun to remind him of the party who took the great-coats last winter. Your bill at last brought and paid, at the rate of sixpence a mouthful, your waiter reproachfully reminds you that "attendance is not charged for a single meal," and you have to search in all your pockets for sixpence more. He has a worse opinion of you than ever, when you have given it to him, and lets you out into the street with the air of one saying to himself, as you cannot doubt he is, "I hope we shall never see *you* here again!"

Or, take any other of the numerous travelling instances in which, with more time at your disposal, you are, have been, or may be, equally ill served. Take the old-established Bull's Head with its old-established knife-boxes on its old-established sideboards, its old-established flue under its old-established four-post bedsteads in its old-established airless rooms, its old-established frouziness up-stairs and down stairs, its old-established cookery, and its old-established principles of plunder. Count up your injuries, in its side-dishes of ailing sweetbreads in white poultices, of apothecaries' powders in rice for curry, of pale stewed bits of calf ineffectually relying for an adventitious interest on forcemeat balls. You have had experience of the old-established Bull's Head's stringy fowls, with lower extremities like wooden legs, sticking up out of the dish; of its cannibalic boiled mutton, gushing horribly among its capers, when carved; of its little dishes of pastry—roofs of spermaceti ointment, erected over half an apple or four gooseberries. Well for you if you have yet forgotten the old-established Bull's Head's fruity port: whose reputation was gained solely by the old-established price the Bull's Head put upon it, and by the old-established air with which the Bull's Head set the glasses and D'Oyleys on, and held that Liquid Gout to the three-and-sixpenny wax-candle, as if its old-established colour hadn't come from the dyer's.

Or lastly, take to finish with, two cases that we all know, every day.

We all know the new hotel near the station, where it is always gusty, going up the lane which is always muddy, where we are sure to arrive at night, and where we make the gas start awfully when we open the front door. We all know the flooring of the passages and staircases that is too new, and the walls that are too new, and the house that is haunted by the ghost of mortar. We all know the doors that have cracked, and the cracked shutters through which we get a glimpse of the disconsolate moon. We all know the new people who have come to keep the new hotel, and who wish they had never come, and who (inevitable result) wish *we* had never come. We all know how much too scant and smooth and bright the new furniture is, and how it has never settled down, and cannot fit itself into right places, and will get into wrong places. We all know how the gas, being lighted, shows maps of Damp upon the walls. We all know how the ghost of mortar passes into our sandwich, stirs our negus, goes up to bed with us, ascends the pale bedroom chimney, and prevents the smoke from following. We all know how a leg of our chair comes off, at breakfast in the morning, and how the dejected waiter attributes the accident to a general greenness pervading the establishment, and informs us, in reply to a local inquiry, that he is thankful to say he is an entire stranger in that part of the country, and is going back to his own connexion on Saturday.

We all know, on the other hand, the great station hotel belonging to the company of proprietors, which has suddenly sprung up in the back outskirts of any place we like to name, and where we look out of our palatial windows, at little back yards and gardens, old summer-houses, fowl-houses, pigeon-traps, and pigsties. We all know this hotel in which we can get anything we want, after its kind, for money; but where nobody is glad to see us, or sorry to see us, or minds (our bill paid) whether we come or go, or how, or when, or why, or cares about us. We all know this hotel, where we have no individuality, but put ourselves into the general post, as it were, and are sorted and disposed of according to our division. We all know that we can get on very well indeed at such a place, but still not perfectly well; and this may be, because the place is largely wholesale, and there is a lingering personal retail interest within us that asks to be satisfied.

To sum up. My uncommercial travelling has not yet brought me to the conclusion that we are close to perfection in these matters. And just as I do not believe that the end of the world will ever be near at hand, so long as any of the very tiresome and arrogant people who constantly predict that catastrophe are left in it, so, I shall have small faith in the Hotel Millennium, while any of the uncomfortable superstitions I have glanced at remain in existence.

VII.

TRAVELLING ABROAD.

I got into the travelling chariot—it was of German make, roomy, heavy, and unvarnished—I got into the travelling chariot, pulled up the steps after me, shut myself in with a smart bang of the door, and gave the word "Go on!"

Immediately, all that W. and S.W. division of London began to slide away at a pace so lively, that I was over the river, and past the Old Kent-road, and out on Blackheath, and even ascending Shooter's Hill, before I had had time to look about me in the carriage, like a collected traveller.

I had two ample Imperials on the roof, other fitted storage for luggage in front, and other up behind; I had a net for books overhead, great pockets to all the windows, a leathern pouch or two hung up for odds and ends, and a reading-lamp fixed in the back of the chariot, in case I should be benighted. I was amply provided in all respects, and had no idea where I was going (which was delightful), except that I was going abroad.

So smooth was the old high road, and so fresh were the

horses, and so fast went I, that it was midway between Gravesend and Rochester, and the widening river was bearing the ships, white-sailed or black-smoked, out to sea, when I noticed by the wayside a very queer small boy.

"Halloa!" said I, to the very queer small boy, "where do you live?"

"At Chatham," says he.

"What do you do there?" says I.

"I go to school," says he.

I took him up in a moment, and we went on. Presently, the very queer small boy says, "This is Gadshill we are coming to, where Falstaff went out to rob those travellers, and ran away."

"You know something about Falstaff, eh?" said I.

"All about him," said the very queer small boy. "I am old (I am nine), and I read all sorts of books. But *do* let us stop at the top of the hill, and look at the house there, if you please!"

"You admire that house?" said I.

"Bless you, sir," said the very queer small boy, "when I was not more than half as old as nine, it used to be a treat for me to be brought to look at it. And now, I am nine, I come by myself to look at it. And ever since I can recollect, my father, seeing me so fond of it, has often said to me, 'If you were to be very persevering and were to work hard, you might some day come to live in it.' Though that's impossible!" said the very queer small boy, drawing a low breath, and now staring at the house out of window with all his might.

I was rather amazed to be told this by the very queer small boy; for that house happens to be *my* house, and I have reason to believe that what he said was true.

Well! I made no halt there, and I soon dropped the very queer small boy and went on. Over the road where the old Romans used to march, over the road where the old Canterbury pilgrims used to go, over the road where the travelling trains of the old imperious priests and princes used to jingle on horseback between the continent and this Island through the mud and water, over the road where Shakespeare hummed to himself, "Blow, blow, thou winter wind," as he sat in the saddle at the gate of the inn yard noticing the carriers; all among the cherry orchards, apple orchards, corn-fields, and hop-gardens; so went I, by Canterbury to Dover. There, the sea was tumbling in, with deep sounds, after dark, and the revolving French light on Cape Grinez was seen regularly bursting out and becoming obscured, as if the head of a gigantic light-keeper in an anxious state of mind were interposed every half minute, to look how it was burning.

Early in the morning I was on the deck of the steam-packet, and we were aiming at the bar in the usual intolerable manner, and the bar was aiming at us in the usual intolerable manner, and the bar got by far the best of it, and we got by far the worst—all in the usual intolerable manner.

But, when I was clear of the Custom House on the other side, and when I began to make the dust fly on the thirsty French roads, and when the twigsome trees by the wayside (which, I suppose, never will grow leafy, for they never did) guarded here and there a dusty soldier, or field labourer, baking on a heap of broken stones, sound asleep in a fiction of shade, I began to recover my travelling spirits. Coming upon the breaker of the broken stones, in a hard hot shining hat, on which the sun played at a distance as on a burning-glass, I felt that now, indeed, I was in the dear old France of my affections. I should have known it, without the well-remembered bottle of rough ordinary wine, the cold roast fowl, the loaf, and the pinch of salt, on which I lunched with unspeakable satisfaction, from one of the stuffed pockets of the chariot.

I must have fallen asleep after lunch, for when a bright face looked in at the window, I started, and said:

"Good God, Louis, I dreamed you were dead!"

My cheerful servant laughed, and answered:

"Me? Not at all, sir."

"How glad I am to wake! What are we doing, Louis?"

"We go to take relay of horses. Will you walk up the hill?"

"Certainly."

Welcome the old French hill, with the old French lunatic (not in the most distant degree related to Sterne's Maria) living in a thatched dog-kennel half way up, and flying out with his crutch and his big head and extended nightcap, to be beforehand with the old men and women exhibiting crippled children, and with the children exhibiting old men and women, ugly and blind, who always seemed by resurrectionary process to be recalled out of the elements for the sudden peopling of the solitude!

"It is well," said I, scattering among them what small coin I had; "here comes Louis, and I am quite roused from my nap."

We journeyed on again, and I welcomed every new assurance that France stood where I had left it. There were the posting-houses, with their archways, dirty stable-yards, and clean post-masters' wives, bright women of business, looking on at the putting-to of the horses; there were the postilions counting what money they got, into their hats, and never making enough of it; there were the standard population of grey horses of Flanders descent, invariably biting one another when they got a chance; there were the fleecy sheepskins, looped on over their uniforms by the postilions, like bibbed aprons, when it blew and rained; there were their jack-boots, and their cracking whips; there were the cathedrals that I got out to see, as under some cruel bondage, in no wise desiring to see them; there were the little towns that appeared to have no reason for being towns, since most of their houses were to let and nobody could be induced to look at them, except the people who couldn't let them and had nothing else to do but look at them all day. I lay a night upon the road and enjoyed delectable cookery of potatoes, and some other sensible things, adoption of which at home would inevitably be shown to be fraught with ruin, somehow or other, to that rickety national blessing, the British farmer; and at last I was rattled, like a single pill in a box, over leagues of stones, until—madly cracking, plunging, and flourishing two grey tails about—I made my triumphal entry into Paris.

At Paris, I took an upper apartment for a few days in one of the hotels of the Rue de Rivoli: my front windows looking into the garden of the Tuileries (where the principal difference between the nursemaids and the flowers seemed to be that the former were locomotive and the latter not): my back windows looking at all the other back windows in the hotel, and deep down into a paved yard, where my German chariot had retired under a tight-fitting archway, to all appearance, for life, and where bells rang all day without anybody's minding them but certain chamberlains with feather brooms and green baize caps, who here and there leaned out of some high window placidly looking down, and where neat waiters with trays on their left shoulders passed and re-passed from morning to night.

Whenever I am at Paris, I am dragged by invisible force into the Morgue. I never want to go there, but am always pulled there. One Christmas Day, when I would rather have been anywhere else, I was attracted in, to see an old grey man lying all alone on his cold bed, with a tap of water turned on over his grey hair, and running, drip, drip, drip, down his wretched face until it got to the corner of his mouth, where it took a turn, and made him look sly. One New Year's Morning (by the same token, the sun was shining outside, and there was a mountebank balancing a feather on his nose, within a yard of the gate), I was pulled in again, to look at a flaxen-haired boy of eighteen with a heart hanging on his breast—" from his mother," was engraven on it—who had come into the net across the river, with a bullet-wound in his fair forehead and his hands cut with a knife, but whence or how was a blank mystery. This time, I was forced into the same dread place, to see a large dark man whose disfigurement by water was in a frightful manner, comic, and whose expression was that of a prize-fighter who had closed his eyelids under a heavy blow, but was going immediately to open them, shake his head, and "come up smiling." O what this large dark man cost me in that bright city!

It was very hot weather, and he was none the better for that, and I was much the worse. Indeed, a very neat and pleasant little woman with the key of her lodging on her forefinger, who had been showing him to her little girl while she and the child ate sweetmeats, observed monsieur looking poorly as we came out together, and asked monsieur, with her wondering little eyebrows prettily raised, if there were anything the matter? Faintly replying in the negative, monsieur crossed the road to a wine-shop, got some brandy, and resolved to freshen himself with a dip in the great floating bath on the river.

The bath was crowded in the usual airy manner, by a male population in striped drawers of various gay colours, who walked up and down arm in arm, drank coffee, smoked cigars, sat at little tables, conversed politely with the damsels who dispensed the towels, and every now and then pitched themselves into the river head foremost, and came out again to repeat this social routine. I made haste to participate in the water part of the entertainments, and was in the full enjoyment of a delightful bath, when all in a moment I was seized with an unreasonable idea that the large dark body was floating straight at me.

I was out of the river, and dressing instantly. In the shock I had taken some water into my mouth, and it turned me sick, for I fancied that the contamination of the creature was in it. I had got back to my cool darkened room in the hotel, and was lying on a sofa there, before I began to reason with myself.

Of course, I knew perfectly well that the large dark creature was stone dead, and that I should no more come upon him out of the place where I had seen him dead, than I should come upon the cathedral of Notre-Dame in an entirely new situation. What troubled me was the picture of the creature; and that had so curiously and strongly painted itself upon my brain, that I could not get rid of it until it was worn out.

I noticed the peculiarities of this possession, while it was a real discomfort to me. That very day, at dinner, some morsel on my plate looked like a piece of him, and I was glad to get up and go out. Later in the evening, I was walking along the Rue St. Honoré, when I saw a bill at a public room there, announcing small-sword exercise, broad-sword exercise, wrestling, and other such feats. I went in, and some of the sword play being very skilful, remained. A specimen of our own national sport, The British Boaxe, was announced to be given at the close of the evening. In an evil hour, I determined to wait for this Boaxe, as became a Briton. It was a clumsy specimen (executed by two English grooms out of place), but, one of the combatants, receiving a straight right-hander with the glove between his eyes, did exactly what the large dark creature in the Morgue had seemed going to do—and finished me for that night.

There was rather a sickly smell (not at all an unusual fragrance in Paris) in the little ante-room of my apartment at the hotel. The large dark creature in the Morgue was by no direct experience associated with my sense of smell, because, when I came to the knowledge of him, he lay behind a wall of thick plate-glass, as good as a wall of steel or marble for that matter. Yet the whiff of the room never failed to reproduce him. What was more curious, was the capriciousness with which his portrait seemed to light itself up in my mind, elsewhere. I might be walking in the Palais Royal, lazily enjoying the shop windows, and might be regaling myself with one of the ready-made clothes shops that are set out there. My eyes, wandering over impossible-waisted dressing-gowns and luminous waistcoats, would fall upon the master, or the shopman, or even the very dummy at the door, and would suggest to me, "Something like him!"—and instantly I was sickened again.

This would happen at the theatre, in the same manner, Often it would happen in the street, when I certainly was not looking for the likeness, and when probably there was no likeness there. It was not because the creature was dead that I was so haunted, because I know that I might have been (and I know it because I have

H

been) equally attended by the image of a living aversion. This lasted about a week. The picture did not fade by degrees, in the sense that it became a whit less forcible and distinct, but in the sense that it obtruded itself less and less frequently. The experience may be worth considering by some who have the care of children. It would be difficult to overstate the intensity and accuracy of an intelligent child's observation. At that impressible time of life, it must sometimes produce a fixed impression. If the fixed impression be of an object terrible to the child, it will be (for want of reasoning upon) inseparable from great fear. Force the child at such a time, be Spartan with it, send it into the dark against its will, leave it in a lonely bedroom against its will, and you had better murder it.

On a bright morning I rattled away from Paris, in the German chariot, and left the large dark creature behind me for good. I ought to confess, though, that I had been drawn back to the Morgue, after he was put under ground, to look at his clothes, and that I found them frightfully like him—particularly his boots. However, I rattled away for Switzerland, looking forward and not backward, and so we parted company.

Welcome again, the long long spell of France, with the queer country inns, full of vases of flowers and clocks, in the dull little towns, and with the little population not at all dull on the little Boulevard in the evening, under the little trees! Welcome Monsieur the Curé walking alone in the early morning a short way out of the town, reading that eternal Breviary of yours, which surely might be almost read, without book, by this time? Welcome Monsieur the Curé, later in the day, jolting through the highway dust (as if you had already ascended to the cloudy region), in a very big-headed cabriolet, with the dried mud of a dozen winters on it. Welcome again Monsieur the Curé, as we exchange salutations: you, straightening your back to look at the German chariot, while picking in your little village garden a vegetable or two for the day's soup: I, looking out of the German chariot window in that delicious traveller's-trance which knows no cares, no yesterdays, no to-morrows, nothing but the passing objects and the passing scents and sounds! And so I came, in due course of delight, to Strasbourg, where I passed a wet Sunday evening at a window, while an idle trifle of a vaudeville was played for me at the opposite house.

How such a large house came to have only three people living in it, was its own affair. There were at least a score of windows in its high roof alone; how many in its grotesque front, I soon gave up counting. The owner was a shopkeeper, by name Straudenheim; by trade—I couldn't make out what by trade, for he had forborne to write that up, and his shop was shut.

At first, as I looked at Straudenheim's, through the steadily falling rain, I set him up in business in the goose-liver line. But, inspection of Straudenheim, who became visible at a window on the second floor, convinced me that there was something more precious than liver in the case. He wore a black velvet skull-cap, and looked usurious and rich. A large-lipped, pear-nosed old man, with white hair, and keen eyes, though near-sighted. He was writing at a desk, was Straudenheim, and ever and again left off writing, put his pen in his mouth, and went through actions with his right hand, like a man steadying piles of cash. Five-franc pieces, Straudenheim, or golden Napoleons? A jeweller, Straudenheim, a dealer in money, a diamond merchant, or what?

Below Straudenheim, at a window on the first floor, sat his housekeeper—far from young, but of a comely presence, suggestive of a well-matured foot and ankle. She was cheerily dressed, had a fan in her hand, and wore large gold earrings and a large gold cross. She would have been out holiday-making (as I settled it) but for the pestilent rain. Strasbourg had given up holiday-making for that once, as a bad job, because the rain was jerking in gushes out of the old roof-spouts, and running in a brook down the middle of the street. The housekeeper, her arms folded on her bosom and her fan tapping her chin, was bright and smiling at her open window, but otherwise Straudenheim's house front was very dreary. The housekeeper's was the only open window in it; Straudenheim kept himself close, though it was a sultry evening when air is pleasant, and though the rain had brought into the town that vague refreshing smell of grass which rain does bring in the summertime.

The dim appearance of a man at Straudenheim's shoulder, inspired me with a misgiving that somebody had come to murder that flourishing merchant for the wealth with which I had handsomely endowed him: the rather, as it was an excited man, lean and long of figure, and evidently stealthy of foot. But, he conferred with Straudenheim instead of doing him a mortal injury, and then they both softly opened the other window of that room—which was immediately over the housekeeper's—and tried to see her by looking down. And my opinion of Straudenheim was much lowered when I saw that eminent citizen spit out of window, clearly with the hope of spitting on the housekeeper.

The unconscious housekeeper fanned herself, tossed her head, and laughed. Though unconscious of Straudenheim, she was conscious of somebody else—of me?—there was nobody else.

After leaning so far out of window, that I confidently expected to see their heels tilt up, Straudenheim and the lean man drew their heads in and shut the window. Presently, the house door secretly opened, and they slowly and spitefully crept forth into the pouring rain. They were coming over to me (I thought) to demand satisfaction for my looking at the housekeeper, when they plunged into a recess in the architecture under my window and dragged out the puniest of little soldiers, begirt with the most innocent of little swords. The tall glazed headdress of this warrior, Straudenheim instantly knocked off, and out of it fell two sugar-sticks, and three or four large lumps of sugar.

The warrior made no effort to recover his property or to pick up his shako, but looked with an expression of attention at Straudenheim when he kicked him five times, and also at the lean man when *he* kicked him five times, and again at Straudenheim when he tore the breast of his (the warrior's) little coat open, and shook all his ten fingers in his face, as if they were ten thousand. When these outrages had been committed, Straudenheim and his man went into the house again and barred the door. A wonderful circumstance was, that the housekeeper who saw it all (and who could have taken six such warriors to her buxom bosom at once), only fanned herself and laughed as she had laughed before, and seemed to have no opinion about it, one way or other.

But, the chief effect of the drama was the remarkable vengeance taken by the little warrior. Left alone in the rain, he picked up his shako; put it on, all wet and dirty as it was; retired into a court, of which Straudenheim's house formed the corner; wheeled about; and bringing his two forefingers close to the top of his nose, rubbed them over one another, crosswise, in derision, defiance, and contempt of Straudenheim. Although Straudenheim could not possibly be supposed to be conscious of this strange proceeding, it so inflated and comforted the little warrior's soul, that twice he went away, and twice came back into the court to repeat it, as though it must goad his enemy to madness. Not only that, but he afterwards came back with two other small warriors, and they all three did it together. Not only that—as I live to tell the tale!—but just as it was falling quite dark, the three came back, bringing with them a huge bearded Sapper, whom they moved, by recital of the original wrong, to go through the same performance, with the same complete absence of all possible knowledge of it on the part of Straudenheim. And then they all went away, arm in arm, singing.

I went away, too, in the German chariot, at sunrise, and rattled on, day after day, like one in a sweet dream; with so many clear little bells on the harness of the horses, that the nursery rhyme about Banbury Cross and the venerable lady who rode in state there, was always in my ears. And now I came to the land of wooden houses, innocent cakes, thin butter soup, and spotless little inn bedrooms with a family likeness to Dairies. And now the Swiss marksmen were for ever rifle-shooting at marks across gorges, so exceedingly near my ear, that I felt like a new Gesler in a Canton of Tells, and went in highly-deserved danger of my tyrannical life. The prizes at these shootings, were watches, smart handkerchiefs, hats, spoons, and (above all) tea-trays; and at these contests I came upon a more than usually accomplished and amiable countryman of my own, who had shot himself deaf in whole years of competition, and had won so many tea-trays that he went about the country with his carriage full of them, like a glorified Cheap-Jack.

In the mountain country into which I had now travelled, a yoke of oxen were sometimes hooked on before the post-horses, and I went lumbering up, up, up, through mist and rain, with the roar of falling water for change of music. Of a sudden, mist and rain would clear away, and I would come down into picturesque little towns with gleaming spires and odd towers; and would stroll afoot into market-places in steep winding streets, where a hundred women in bodices, sold eggs and honey, butter and fruit, and suckled their children as they sat by their clean baskets, and had such enormous goitres (or glandular swellings in the throat) that it became a science to know where the nurse ended and the child began. About this time, I deserted my German chariot for the back of a mule (in colour and consistency so very like a dusty old hair trunk I once had at school, that I half expected to see my initials in brass-headed nails on his backbone), and went up a thousand rugged ways, and looked down at a thousand woods of fir and pine, and would on the whole have preferred my mule's keeping a little nearer to the inside, and not usually travelling with a hoof or two over the precipice—though much consoled by explanation that this was to be attributed to his great sagacity, by reason of his carrying broad loads of wood at other times, and not being clear but that I myself belonged to that station of life, and required as much room as they. He brought me safely, in his own wise way, among the passes of the Alps, and here I enjoyed a dozen climates a day; being now (like Don Quixote on the back of the wooden horse) in the region of wind, now in the region of fire, now in the region of unmelting ice and snow. Here, I passed over trembling domes of ice, beneath which the cataract was roaring; and here was received under arches of icicles, of unspeakable beauty; and here the sweet air was so bracing and so light, that at halting-times I rolled in the snow when I saw my mule do it, thinking that he must know best. At this part of the journey we would come, at mid-day, into half an hour's thaw: when the rough mountain inn would be found on an island of deep mud in a sea of snow, while the baiting strings of mules, and the carts full of casks and bales, which had been in an Arctic condition a mile off, would steam again. By such ways and means, I would come to the cluster of châlets where I had to turn out of the track to see the waterfall; and then, uttering a howl like a young giant, on espying a traveller—in other words, something to eat—coming up the steep, the idiot lying on the wood-pile who sunned himself and nursed his goitre, would rouse the woman-guide within the hut, who would stream out hastily, throwing her child over one of her shoulders and her goitre over the other, as she came along. I slept at religious houses, and bleak refuges of many kinds, on this journey, and by the stove at night heard stories of travellers who had perished within call, in wreaths and drifts of snow. One night the stove within, and the cold outside, awakened childish associations long forgotten, and I dreamed I was in Russia—the identical serf out of a picture-book I had, before I could read it for myself—and that I was going to be knouted by a noble personage in a fur cap, boots, and earrings, who, I think, must have come out of some melodrama.

Commend me to the beautiful waters among these mountains! Though I was not of their mind: they, being inveterately bent on getting down into the level country, and I ardently desiring to linger where I was. What desperate leaps they took, what dark abysses they plunged into, what rocks they wore away, what echoes they invoked! In one part where I went, they were pressed into the service of carrying wood down, to be burnt next winter, as costly fuel, in Italy. But, their fierce savage nature was not to be easily constrained, and they fought with every limb of the wood; whirling it round and round, stripping its bark away, dashing it against pointed corners, driving it out of the course, and roaring and flying at the peasants who steered it back again from the bank with long stout poles. Alas! concurrent streams of time and water carried *me* down fast, and I came, on an exquisitely clear day, to the Lausanne shore of the Lake of Geneva, where I stood looking at the bright blue water, the flushed white mountains opposite, and the boats at my feet with their furled Mediterranean sails, showing like enormous magnifications of this goose-quill pen that is now in my hand.

—The sky became overcast without any notice; a wind very like the March east wind of England, blew across me; and a voice said, "How do you like it? Will it do?"

I had merely shut myself, for half a minute, in a German travelling chariot that stood for sale in the Carriage Department of the London Pantechnicon. I had a commission to buy it, for a friend who was going abroad; and the look and manner of the chariot, as I tried the cushions and the springs, brought all these hints of travelling remembrance before me.

"It will do very well," said I, rather sorrowfully, as I got out at the other door, and shut the carriage up.

VIII.

THE GREAT TASMANIA'S CARGO.

I TRAVEL constantly, up and down a certain line of railway that has a terminus in London. It is the railway for a large military depôt, and for other large barracks. To the best of my serious belief, I have never been on that railway by daylight, without seeing some handcuffed deserters in the train.

It is in the nature of things that such an institution as our English army should have many bad and troublesome characters in it. But, this is a reason for, and not against, its being made as acceptable as possible to well-disposed men of decent behaviour. Such men are assuredly not tempted into the ranks, by the beastly inversion of natural laws, and the compulsion to live in worse than swinish foulness. Accordingly, when any such Circumlocutional embellishments of the soldier's condition have of late been brought to notice, we civilians, seated in outer darkness cheerfully meditating on an Income Tax, have considered the matter as being our business, and have shown a tendency to declare that we would rather not have it misregulated, if such declaration may, without violence to the Church Catechism, be hinted to those who are put in authority over us.

Any animated description of a modern battle, any private soldier's letter published in the newspapers, any page of the records of the Victoria Cross, will show that in the ranks of the army, there exists under all disadvantages as fine a sense of duty as is to be found in any station on earth. Who doubts that if we all did our duty as faithfully as the soldier does his, this world would be a better place? There may be greater difficulties in our way than in the soldier's. Not disputed. But, let us at least do our duty towards *him*.

I had got back again to that rich and beautiful port where I had looked after Mercantile Jack, and I was walking up a hill there, on a wild March morning. My conversation with my official friend Pangloss, by whom I was accidentally accompanied, took this direction as we took the up-hill direction, because the object of my uncommercial journey was to see some discharged soldiers who had recently come home from India. There were men of HAVELOCK's among them; there were men who had been in many of the great battles of the great Indian campaign, among them; and I was curious to note what our discharged soldiers looked like, when they were done with.

I was not the less interested (as I mentioned to my official friend Pangloss) because these men had claimed to be discharged, when their right to be discharged was not admitted. They had behaved with unblemished fidelity and bravery; but, a change of circumstances had

CIRCUMLOCUTION OFFICE (PAGODA DEPARTMENT). 109

arisen, which, as they considered, put an end to their compact and entitled them to enter on a new one. Their demand had been blunderingly resisted by the authorities in India; but, it is to be presumed that the men were not far wrong, inasmuch as the bungle had ended in their being sent home discharged, in pursuance of orders from home. (There was an immense waste of money, of course.)

Under these circumstances—thought I, as I walked up the hill, on which I accidentally encountered my official friend—under these circumstances of the men having successfully opposed themselves to the Pagoda Department of that great Circumlocution Office on which the sun never sets and the light of reason never rises, the Pagoda Department will have been particularly careful of the national honour. It will have shown these men, in the scrupulous good faith, not to say the generosity, of its dealing with them, that great national authorities can have no small retaliations and revenges. It will have made every provision for their health on the passage home, and will have landed them, restored from their campaigning fatigues by a sea-voyage, pure air, sound food, and good medicines. And I pleased myself with dwelling beforehand, on the great accounts of their personal treatment which these men would carry into their various towns and villages, and on the increasing popularity of the service that would insensibly follow. I almost began to hope that the hitherto-never-failing deserters on my railroad, would by-and-by become a phenomenon.

In this agreeable frame of mind I entered the workhouse of Liverpool.—For, the cultivation of laurels in a sandy soil, had brought the soldiers in question to *that* abode of Glory.

Before going into their wards to visit them, I inquired how they had made their triumphant entry there? They had been brought through the rain in carts, it seemed, from the landing-place to the gate, and had then been carried up-stairs on the backs of paupers. Their groans and pains during the performance of this glorious pageant, had been so distressing, as to bring tears into the eyes of spectators but too well accustomed to scenes of suffering. The men were so dreadfully cold, that those who could get near the fires were hard to be restrained from thrusting their feet in among the blazing coals. They were so horribly reduced, that they were awful to look upon. Racked with dysentery and blackened with scurvy, one hundred and forty wretched soldiers had been revived with brandy and laid in bed.

My official friend Pangloss is lineally descended from a learned doctor of that name, who was once tutor to Candide, an ingenious young gentleman of some celebrity. In his personal character, he is as humane and worthy a gentleman as any I know; in his official capacity, he unfortunately preaches the doctrines of his renowned ancestor, by demonstrating on all occasions that we live in the best of all possible official worlds.

"In the name of Humanity," said I, "how did the men fall into this deplorable state? Was the ship well found in stores?"

"I am not here to asseverate that I know the fact, of my own knowledge," answered Pangloss, "but I have grounds for asserting that the stores were the best of all possible stores."

A medical officer laid before us, a handful of rotten biscuit, and a handful of split peas. The biscuit was a honeycombed heap of maggots, and the excrement of maggots. The peas were even harder than this filth. A similar handful had been experimentally boiled, six hours, and had shown no signs of softening. These were the stores on which the soldiers had been fed.

"The beef——" I began, when Pangloss cut me short.

"Was the best of all possible beef," said he.

But, behold, there was laid before us certain evidence given at the Coroner's Inquest, holden on some of the men (who had obstinately died of their treatment), and from that evidence it appeared that the beef was the worst of all possible beef!

"Then I lay my hand upon my heart, and take my stand," said Pangloss, "by the pork, which was the best of all possible pork."

"But look at this food before our eyes, if one may so misuse the word," said I. "Would any Inspector who did his duty, pass such abomination?"

"It ought not to have been passed," Pangloss admitted.

"Then the authorities out there——" I began, when Pangloss cut me short again.

"There would certainly seem to have been something

wrong somewhere," said he; "but I am prepared to prove that the authorities out there, are the best of all possible authorities."

I never heard of any impeached public authority in my life, who was not the best public authority in existence.

"We are told of these unfortunate men being laid low by scurvy," said I. "Since lime-juice has been regularly stored and served out in our navy, surely that disease, which used to devastate it, has almost disappeared? Was there lime-juice aboard this transport?"

My official friend was beginning "the best of all possible——" when an inconvenient medical forefinger pointed out another passage in the evidence, from which it appeared that the lime-juice had been bad too. Not to mention that the vinegar had been bad too, the vegetables bad too, the cooking accommodation insufficient (if there had been anything worth mentioning to cook), the water supply exceedingly inadequate, and the beer sour.

"Then, the men," said Pangloss, a little irritated, "were the worst of all possible men."

"In what respect?" I asked.

"Oh! Habitual drunkards," said Pangloss.

But, again the same incorrigible medical forefinger pointed out another passage in the evidence, showing that the dead men had been examined after death, and that they, at least, could not possibly have been habitual drunkards, because the organs within them which must have shown traces of that habit, were perfectly sound.

"And besides," said the three doctors present, one and

all, "habitual drunkards brought as low as these men have been, could not recover under care and food, as the great majority of these men are recovering. They would not have strength of constitution to do it."

"Reckless and improvident dogs, then," said Pangloss. "Always are—nine times out of ten."

I turned to the master of the workhouse, and asked him whether the men had any money?

"Money?" said he. "I have in my iron safe, nearly four hundred pounds of theirs; the agents have nearly a hundred pounds more; and many of them have left money in Indian banks besides."

"Hah!" said I to myself, as we went up-stairs, "this is not the best of all possible stories, I doubt!"

We went into a large ward, containing some twenty or five-and-twenty beds. We went into several such wards, one after another. I find it very difficult to indicate what a shocking sight I saw in them, without frightening the reader from the perusal of these lines, and defeating my object of making it known.

O the sunken eyes that turned to me as I walked between the rows of beds, or—worse still—that glazedly looked at the white ceiling, and saw nothing and cared for nothing! Here, lay the skeleton of a man, so lightly covered with a thin unwholesome skin, that not a bone in the anatomy was clothed, and I could clasp the arm above the elbow, in my finger and thumb. Here, lay a man with the black scurvy eating his legs away, his gums gone, and his teeth all gaunt and bare. This bed was empty, because gangrene had set in, and the patient had died but yesterday. That bed was a hopeless one, because its occupant was sinking fast, and could only be roused to turn the poor pinched mask of face upon the pillow, with a feeble moan. The awful thinness of the fallen cheeks, the awful brightness of the deep-set eyes, the lips of lead, the hands of ivory, the recumbent human images lying in the shadow of death with a kind of solemn twilight on them, like the sixty who had died aboard the ship and were lying at the bottom of the sea, O Pangloss, GOD forgive you!

In one bed, lay a man whose life had been saved (as it was hoped) by deep incisions in the feet and legs. While I was speaking to him, a nurse came up to change the poultices which this operation had rendered necessary, and I had an instinctive feeling that it was not well to turn away, merely to spare myself. He was sorely wasted and keenly susceptible, but the efforts he made to subdue any expression of impatience or suffering, were quite heroic. It was easy to see, in the shrinking of the figure, and the drawing of the bed-clothes over the head, how acute the endurance was, and it made me shrink too, as if *I* were in pain; but, when the new bandages were on, and the poor feet were composed again, he made an apology for himself (though he had not uttered a word), and said plaintively, "I am so tender and weak, you see, sir!" Neither from him nor from any one sufferer of the whole ghastly number, did I hear a complaint. Of thankfulness for present solicitude and care, I heard much; of complaint, not a word.

I think I could have recognised in the dismalest skeleton there, the ghost of a soldier. Something of the old air was still latent in the palest shadow of life I talked to. One emaciated creature, in the strictest literality worn to the bone, lay stretched on his back, looking so like death that I asked one of the doctors if he were not dying, or dead? A few kind words from the doctor, in his ear, and he opened his eyes, and smiled—looked, in a moment, as if he would have made a salute, if he could. "We shall pull him through, please God," said the Doctor. "Plase God, surr, and thankye," said the patient. "You are much better to-day; are you not?" said the Doctor. "Plase God, surr; 'tis the slape I want, surr; 'tis my breathin' makes the nights so long." "He is a careful fellow this, you must know," said the Doctor, cheerfully; "it was raining hard when they put him in the open cart to bring him here, and he had the presence of mind to ask to have a sovereign taken out of his pocket that he had there, and a cab engaged. Probably it saved his life." The patient rattled out the skeleton of a laugh, and said, proud of the story, "'Deed, surr, an open cairt was a comical means o' bringin' a dyin' man here, and a clever way to kill him." You might have sworn to him for a soldier when he said it.

One thing had perplexed me very much in going from bed to bed. A very significant and cruel thing. I could find no young man, but one. He had attracted my notice, by having got up and dressed himself in his soldier's jacket and trousers, with the intention of sitting by the fire; but he had found himself too weak, and had crept back to his bed and laid himself down on the outside of it. I could have pronounced him, alone, to be a young man aged by famine and sickness. As we were standing by the Irish soldier's bed, I mentioned my perplexity to the Doctor. He took a board with an inscription on it from the head of the Irishman's bed, and asked me what age I supposed that man to be? I had observed him with attention while talking to him, and answered, confidently, "Fifty." The doctor, with a pitying glance at the patient, who had dropped into a stupor again, put the board back, and said, "Twenty-Four."

All the arrangements of the wards were excellent. They could not have been more humane, sympathising, gentle, attentive, or wholesome. The owners of the ship, too, had done all they could, liberally. There were bright fires in every room, and the convalescent men were sitting round them, reading various papers and periodicals. I took the liberty of inviting my official friend Pangloss to look at those convalescent men, and to tell me whether their faces and bearing were or were not, generally, the faces and bearing of steady respectable soldiers? The master of the workhouse, overhearing me, said he had had a pretty large experience of troops, and that better conducted men than these, he had never had to do with. They were always (he added) as we saw them. And of us visitors (I add) they knew nothing whatever, except that we were there.

It was audacious in me, but I took another liberty with Pangloss. Prefacing it with the observation that, of course, I knew beforehand that there was not the faintest desire, anywhere, to hush up any part of this dreadful business, and that the Inquest was the fairest of all possible Inquests, I besought four things of Pangloss. Firstly, to observe that the Inquest *was not held in that place*, but at some distance off. Secondly, to look round upon those helpless spectres in their beds. Thirdly, to remember that the witnesses produced from among them before that Inquest, could not have been selected because they were the men who had the most to tell it, but because they happened to be in a state admitting of their safe removal. Fourthly, to say whether the coroner and Jury could have come there, to those pillows, and taken a little evidence? My official friend declined to commit himself to a reply.

There was a sergeant, reading, in one of the fireside groups. As he was a man of a very intelligent countenance, and as I have a great respect for non-commissioned officers as a class, I sat down on the nearest bed, to have some talk with him. (It was the bed of one of the grisliest of the poor skeletons, and he died soon afterwards.)

"I was glad to see, in the evidence of an officer at the Inquest, sergeant, that he never saw men behave better on board ship than these men."

"They did behave very well, sir."

"I was glad to see, too, that every man had a hammock."

The sergeant gravely shook his head. "There must be some mistake, sir. The men of my own mess had no hammocks. There were not hammocks enough on board, and the men of the two next messes laid hold of hammocks for themselves as soon as they got on board, and squeezed my men out, as I may say."

"Had the squeezed-out men none then?"

"None, sir. As men died, their hammocks were used by other men, who wanted hammocks; but many men had none at all."

"Then you don't agree with the evidence on that point?"

"Certainly not, sir. A man can't, when he knows to the contrary."

"Did any of the men sell their bedding for drink?"

"There is some mistake on that point too, sir. Men were under the impression—I knew it for a fact at the time—that it was not allowed to take blankets or bedding on board, and so men who had things of that sort came to sell them purposely."

"Did any of the men sell their clothes for drink?"

"They did, sir." (I believe there never was a more truthful witness than the sergeant. He had no inclination to make out a case.)

"Many?"

"Some, sir" (considering the question). "Soldier-like. They had been long marching in the rainy season, by bad roads—no roads at all, in short—and when they got to Calcutta, men turned to and drank, before taking a last look at it. Soldier-like."

"Do you see any men in this ward, for example, who sold clothes for drink at that time?"

The sergeant's wan eye, happily just beginning to rekindle with health, travelled round the place and came back to me. "Certainly, sir."

"The marching to Calcutta in the rainy season must have been severe?"

"It was very severe, sir."

"Yet what with the rest and the sea air, I should have thought that the men (even the men who got drunk) would have soon begun to recover on board ship?"

"So they might; but the bad food told upon them, and when we got into a cold latitude, it began to tell more, and the men dropped."

"The sick had a general disinclination for food, I am told, Sergeant?"

"Have you seen the food, sir?"

"Some of it."

"Have you seen the state of their mouths, sir?"

If the sergeant, who was a man of a few orderly words, had spoken the amount of this volume, he could not have settled that question better. I believe the sick could as soon have eaten the ship, as the ship's provisions.

I took the additional liberty with my friend Pangloss, when I had left the sergeant with good wishes, of asking Pangloss whether he had ever heard of biscuit getting drunk and bartering its nutritious qualities for putrefaction and vermin; of peas becoming hardened in liquor; of hammocks drinking themselves off the face of the earth; of lime-juice, vegetables, vinegar, cooking accommodation, water supply, and beer, all taking to drinking together and going to ruin? "If not (I asked him), what did he say in defence of the officers condemned by the Coroner's Jury, who, by signing the General Inspection report relative to the ship Great Tasmania chartered for these troops, had deliberately asserted all that bad and poisonous dunghill refuse, to be good and wholesome food? My official friend replied that it was a remarkable fact, that whereas some officers were only positively good, and other officers only comparatively better, those particular officers were superlatively the very best of all possible officers.

My hand and my heart fail me, in writing my record of this journey. The spectacle of the soldiers in the hospital-beds of that Liverpool workhouse (a very good workhouse, indeed, be it understood), was so shocking and so shameful, that as an Englishman I blush to remember it. It would have been simply unbearable at the time, but for the consideration and pity with which they were soothed in their sufferings.

No punishment that our inefficient laws provide, is worthy of the name when set against the guilt of this transaction. But, if the memory of it die out unavenged, and if it do not result in the inexorable dismissal and disgrace of those who are responsible for it, their escape will be infamous to the Government (no matter of what party) that so neglects its duty, and infamous to the nation that tamely suffers such intolerable wrong to be done in its name.

IX.

CITY OF LONDON CHURCHES.

If the confession that I have often travelled from this Covent Garden lodging of mine on Sundays, should give offence to those who never travel on Sundays, they will be satisfied (I hope) by my adding that the journeys in question were made to churches.

Not that I have any curiosity to hear powerful preachers. Time was, when I was dragged by the hair of my head, as one may say, to hear too many. On summer evenings, when every flower, and tree, and bird, might have better addressed my soft young heart, I have in my day been caught in the palm of a female hand by the crown, have been violently scrubbed from the neck to the roots of the hair as a purification for the Temple, and have then been carried off highly charged with saponaceous electricity, to be steamed like a potato in the unventilated breath of the powerful Boanerges Boiler and his congregation, until what small mind I had, was quite steamed out of me. In which pitiable plight I have been haled out of the place of meeting, at the conclusion of the exercises, and catechised respecting Boanerges Boiler, his fifthly, his sixthly, and his seventhly, until I have regarded that reverend person in the light of a most dismal and oppressive Charade. Time was, when I was carried off to platform assemblages at which no human child, whether of wrath or grace, could possibly keep its eyes open, and when I felt the fatal sleep stealing, stealing over me, and when I gradually heard the orator in possession, spinning and humming like a great top, until he rolled, collapsed, and tumbled over, and I discovered to my burning shame and fear, that as to that last stage it was not he, but I. I have sat under Boanerges when he has specifically addressed himself to us —us, the infants—and at this present writing I hear his lumbering jocularity (which never amused us, though we basely pretended that it did), and I behold his big round face, and I look up the inside of his outstretched coat-sleeve as if it were a telescope with the stopper on, and I hate him with an unwholesome hatred for two hours. Through such means did it come to pass that I knew the powerful preacher from beginning to end, all over and all through, while I was very young, and that I left him behind at an early period of life. Peace be with him! More peace than he brought to me!

Now, I have heard many preachers since that time— not powerful; merely Christian, unaffected, and reverential—and I have had many such preachers on my roll of friends. But, it was not to hear these, any more than the powerful class, that I made my Sunday journeys. They were journeys of curiosity to the numerous churches in the City of London. It came into my head one day, here had I been cultivating a familiarity with all the churches of Rome, and I knew nothing of the insides of the old churches of London! This befel on a Sunday morning. I began my expeditions that very same day, and they lasted me a year.

I never wanted to know the names of the churches to which I went, and to this hour I am profoundly ignorant in that particular of at least nine-tenths of them. Indeed, saving that I know the church of old GOWER's tomb (he lies in effigy with his head upon his books) to be the church of Saint Saviour's, Southwark; and the church of MILTON's tomb to be the church of Cripplegate; and the church on Cornhill with the great golden keys to be the church of Saint Peter; I doubt if I could pass a competitive examination in any of the names. No question did I ever ask of living creature concerning these churches, and no answer to any antiquarian question on the subject that I ever put to books, shall harass the reader's soul. A full half of my pleasure in them arose out of their mystery; mysterious I found them; mysterious they shall remain for me.

Where shall I begin my round of hidden and forgotten old churches in the City of London?

It is twenty minutes short of eleven on a Sunday morning, when I stroll down one of the many narrow hilly streets in the City that tend due south to the Thames. It is my first experiment, and I have come to the region of Whittington in an omnibus, and we have put down a fierce-eyed spare old woman, whose slate-coloured gown smells of herbs, and who walked up

Aldersgate-street to some chapel where she comforts herself with brimstone doctrine, I warrant. We have also put down a stouter and sweeter old lady, with a pretty large prayer-book in an unfolded pocket-handkerchief, who got out at a corner of a court near Stationers' Hall, and who I think must go to church there, because she is the widow of some deceased Old Company's Beadle. The rest of our freight were mere chance pleasure-seekers and rural walkers, and went on to the Blackwall railway. So many bells are ringing, when I stand undecided at a street corner, that every sheep in the ecclesiastical fold might be a bell-wether. The discordance is fearful. My state of indecision is referable to, and about equally divisible among, four great churches, which are all within sight and sound, all within the space of a few square yards. As I stand at the street corner, I don't see as many as four people at once going to church, though I see as many as four churches with their steeples clamouring for people. I choose my church, and go up the flight of steps to the great entrance in the tower. A mouldy tower within, and like a neglected washhouse. A rope comes through the beamed roof, and a man in the corner pulls it and clashes the bell—a whity-brown man, whose clothes were once black—a man with flue on him, and cobweb. He stares at me, wondering how I come there, and I stare at him, wondering how he comes there. Through a screen of wood and glass, I peep into the dim church. About twenty people are discernible, waiting to begin. Christening would seem to have faded out of this church long ago, for the font has the dust of desuetude thick upon it, and its wooden cover (shaped like an old-fashioned tureen-cover) looks as if it wouldn't come off, upon requirement. I perceive the altar to be rickety, and the Commandments damp. Entering after this survey, I jostle the clergyman in his canonicals, who is entering too from a dark lane behind a pew of state with curtains, where nobody sits. The pew is ornamented with four blue wands, once carried by four somebodys, I suppose, before somebody else, but which there is nobody now to hold or receive honour from. I open the door of a family pew, and shut myself in; if I could occupy twenty family pews at once, I might have them. The clerk, a brisk young man (how does *he* come here?), glances at me knowingly, as who should say, " You have done it now; you must stop." Organ plays. Organ-loft is in a small gallery across the church; gallery congregation, two girls. I wonder within myself what will happen when we are required to sing.

There is a pale heap of books in the corner of my pew, and while the organ, which is hoarse and sleepy, plays in such fashion that I can hear more of the rusty working of the stops than of any music, I look at the books, which are mostly bound in faded baize and stuff. They belonged in 1754, to the Dowgate family; and who were they? Jane Comport must have married Young Dowgate, and come into the family that way; Young Dowgate was courting Jane Comport when he gave her her prayer-book, and recorded the presentation in the flyleaf; if Jane were fond of Young Dowgate, why did she die and leave the book here? Perhaps at the rickety altar, and before the damp Commandments, she, Comport, had taken him, Dowgate, in a flush of youthful hope and joy, and perhaps it had not turned out in the long run as great a success as was expected?

The opening of the service recals my wandering thoughts. I then find, to my astonishment, that I have been, and still am, taking a strong kind of invisible snuff, up my nose, into my eyes, and down my throat. I wink, sneeze, and cough. The clerk sneezes; the clergyman winks; the unseen organist sneezes and coughs (and probably winks); all our little party wink, sneeze, and cough. The snuff seems to be made of the decay of matting, wood, cloth, stone, iron, earth, and something else. Is the something else, the decay of dead citizens in the vaults below? As sure as Death it is! Not only in the cold damp February day, do we cough and sneeze dead citizens, all through the service, but dead citizens have got into the very bellows of the organ, and half choked the same. We stamp our feet to warm them, and dead citizens arise in heavy clouds. Dead citizens stick upon the walls, and lie pulverised on the sounding-board over the clergyman's head, and, when a gust of air comes, tumble down upon him.

In this first experience I was so nauseated by too much snuff, made of the Dowgate family, the Comport branch, and other families and branches, that I gave but little heed to our dull manner of ambling through the service; to the brisk clerk's manner of encouraging us to try a note or two at psalm time; to the gallery-congregation's manner of enjoying a shrill duet, without a notion of time or tune; to the whity-brown man's manner of shutting the minister into the pulpit, and being very particular with the lock of the door, as if he were a dangerous animal. But, I tried again next Sunday, and soon accustomed myself to the dead citizens when I found that I could not possibly get on without them among the City churches.

Another Sunday.
After being again rung for by conflicting bells, like a leg of mutton or a laced hat a hundred years ago, I make selection of a church oddly put away in a corner among a number of lanes—a smaller church than the last, and an ugly: of about the date of Queen Anne. As a congregation, we are fourteen strong: not counting an exhausted charity school in a gallery, which has dwindled away to four boys, and two girls. In the porch, is a benefaction of loaves of bread, which there would seem to be nobody left in the exhausted congregation to claim, and which I saw an exhausted beadle, long faded out of uniform, eating with his eyes for self and family when I passed in. There is also an exhausted clerk in a brown wig, and two or three exhausted doors and windows have been bricked up, and the service books are musty, and the pulpit cushions are threadbare, and the whole of the church furniture is in a very advanced stage of exhaustion. We are three old women (habitual), two young lovers (accidental), two tradesmen, one with a wife and one alone, an aunt and nephew, again two girls (these two girls dressed out for

church with everything about them limp that should be stiff, and *vice versâ*, are an invariable experience), and three sniggering boys. The clergyman is, perhaps, the chaplain of a civic company; he has the moist and vinous look, and eke the bulbous boots, of one acquainted with 'Twenty port, and comet vintages.

We are so quiet in our dulness that the three sniggering boys, who have got away into a corner by the altar-railing, give us a start, like crackers, whenever they laugh. And this reminds me of my own village church where, during sermon-time on bright Sundays when the birds are very musical indeed, farmers' boys patter out over the stone pavement, and the clerk steps out from his desk after them, and is distinctly heard in the summer repose to pursue and punch them in the churchyard, and is seen to return with a meditative countenance, making believe that nothing of the sort has happened. The aunt and nephew in this City church are much disturbed by the sniggering boys. The nephew is himself a boy, and the sniggerers tempt him to secular thoughts of marbles and string, by secretly offering such commodities to his distant contemplation. This young Saint Anthony for a while resists, but presently becomes a backslider, and in dumb show defies the sniggerers to "heave" a marble or two in his direction. Herein he is detected by the aunt (a rigorous reduced gentlewoman who has the charge of offices), and I perceive that worthy relative to poke him in the side, with the corrugated hooked handle of an ancient umbrella. The nephew revenges himself for this, by holding his breath and terrifying his kinswoman with the dread belief that he has made up his mind to burst. Regardless of whispers and shakes, he swells and becomes discoloured, and yet again swells and becomes discoloured, until the aunt can bear it no longer, but leads him out, with no visible neck, and with his eyes going before him like a prawn's. This causes the sniggerers to regard flight as an eligible move, and I know which of them will go out first, because of the over-devout attention that he suddenly concentrates on the clergyman. In a little while, this hypocrite, with an elaborate demonstration of hushing his footsteps, and with a face generally expressive of having until now forgotten a religious appointment elsewhere, is gone. Number two gets out in the same way, but rather quicker. Number three getting safely to the door, there turns reckless, and banging it open, flies forth with a Whoop! that vibrates to the top of the tower above us.

The clergyman, who is of a prandial presence and a muffled voice, may be scant of hearing as well as of breath, but he only glances up, as having an idea that somebody has said Amen in a wrong place, and continues his steady jog-trot, like a farmer's wife going to market. He does all he has to do, in the same easy way, and gives us a concise sermon, still like the jog-trot of the farmer's wife on a level road. Its drowsy cadence soon lulls the three old women asleep, and the unmarried tradesman sits looking out at window, and the married tradesman sits looking at his wife's bonnet, and the lovers sit looking at one another, so superlatively happy, that I mind when I, turned of eighteen, went with my Angelica to a City church on account of a shower (by this special coincidence that it was in Huggin-lane), and when I said to my Angelica, " Let the blessed event, Angelica, occur at no altar but this!" and when my Angelica consented that it should occur at no other—which it certainly never did, for it never occurred anywhere. And O, Angelica, what has become of you, this present Sunday morning when I can't attend to the sermon; and, more difficult question than that, what has become of Me as I was when I sat by your side!

But, we receive the signal to make that unanimous dive which surely is a little conventional—like the strange rustlings and settlings and clearings of throats and noses, which are never dispensed with, at certain points of the Church service, and are never held to be necessary under any other circumstances. In a minute more it is all over, and the organ expresses itself to be as glad of it as it can be of anything in its rheumatic state, and in another minute we are all of us out of the church, and Whity-brown has locked it up. Another minute or little more, and, in the neighbouring churchyard—not the yard of that church, but of another—a churchyard like a great shabby old mignionette-box, with two trees in it and one tomb—I meet Whity-brown, in his private capacity, fetching a pint of beer for his dinner from the public-house in the corner, where the keys of the rotting fire-ladders are kept and were never asked for, and where there is a ragged, white-seamed, out-at-elbowed bagatelle-board on the first floor.

In one of these City churches, and only in one, I found an individual who might have been claimed as expressly a City personage. I remember the church, by the feature that the clergyman couldn't get to his own desk without going through the clerk's, or couldn't get to the pulpit without going through the reading-desk—I forget which, and it is no matter—and by the presence of this personage among the exceedingly sparse congregation. I doubt if we were a dozen, and we had no exhausted charity school to help us out. The personage was dressed in black of square cut, and was stricken in years, and wore a black velvet cap, and cloth shoes. He was of a staid, wealthy, and dissatisfied aspect. In his hand, he conducted to church a mysterious child: a child of the feminine gender. The child had a beaver hat, with a stiff drab plume that surely never belonged to any bird of the air. The child was further attired in a nankeen frock and spencer, brown boxing-gloves, and a veil. It had a blemish, in the nature of current jelly, on its chin; and was a thirsty child. Insomuch that the personage carried in his pocket a green bottle, from which, when the first psalm was given out, the child was openly refreshed. At all other times throughout the service it was motionless, and stood on the seat of the large pew, closely fitted into the corner, like a rain-water pipe.

The personage never opened his book, and never looked at the clergyman. *He* never sat down either, but stood with his arms leaning on the top of the pew, and his forehead sometimes shaded with his right hand, always looking at the church door. It was a long church for a church of its size, and he was at the upper end, but he always looked at the door. That he was an old bookkeeper, or an old trader who had kept his own books, and that he might be seen at the Bank of England about Dividend times, no doubt. That he had lived in the City all his life and was disdainful of other localities, no doubt. Why he looked at the door, I never absolutely proved, but it is my belief that he lived in expectation of the time when the citizens would come back to live in the City, and its ancient glories would be renewed. He appeared to expect that this would occur on a Sunday, and that the wanderers would first appear, in the deserted churches, penitent and humbled. Hence, he looked at the door which they never darkened. Whose child the child was, whether the child of a disinherited daughter, or some parish orphan whom the personage had adopted, there was nothing to lead up to. It never played, or skipped, or smiled. Once, the idea occurred to me that it was an automaton, and that the personage had made it; but following the strange couple out one Sunday, I heard the personage say to it, "Thirteen thousand pounds;" to which it added in a weak human voice, " Seventeen and fourpence." Four Sundays, I followed them out, and this is all I ever heard or saw them say. One Sunday, I followed them home. They lived behind a pump, and the personage opened their abode with an exceeding large key. The one solitary inscription on their house related to a fire-plug. The house was partly undermined by a deserted and closed gateway; its windows were blind with dirt; and it stood with its face disconsolately turned to a wall. Five great churches and two small ones rang their Sunday bells between this house and the church the couple frequented, so they must have had some special reason for going a quarter of a mile to it. The last time I saw them, was on this wise. I had been to explore another church at a distance, and happened to pass the church they frequented, at about two of the afternoon when that edifice was closed. But, a little side-door, which I had never observed before, stood open, and disclosed certain cellarous steps. Methought, "They are airing the vaults to-day," when the personage and the child silently arrived at the steps, and silently descended. Of course, I came to the conclusion that the personage had at last despaired of the looked-for return of the penitent citizens, and that he and the child went down to get themselves buried.

In the course of my pilgrimages I came upon one obscure church which had broken out in the melodramatic style, and was got up with various tawdry decorations, much after the manner of the extinct London maypoles. These attractions had induced several young priests or deacons in black bibs for waistcoats, and several young ladies interested in that holy order (the proportion being, as I estimated, seventeen young ladies to a deacon), to come into the City as a new and odd excitement. It was wonderful to see how these young people played out their little play in the heart of the City, all among themselves, without the deserted City's knowing anything about it. It was as if you should take an empty counting-house on a Sunday, and act one of the old Mysteries there. They had impressed a small school (from what neighbourhood I don't know) to assist in the performances, and it was pleasant to notice frantic garlands of inscription on the walls, especially addressing those poor innocents in characters impossible for them to decipher. There was a remarkably agreeable smell of pomatum in this congregation.

But, in other cases, rot and mildew and dead citizens formed the uppermost scent, while, infused into it in a dreamy way not at all displeasing, was the staple character of the neighbourhood. In the churches about Mark-lane, for example, there was a dry whiff of wheat; and I accidentally struck an airy sample of barley out of an aged hassock in one of them. From Rood-lane to Tower-street, and thereabouts, there was often a subtle flavour of wine: sometimes, of tea. One church near Mincing-lane smelt like a druggist's drawer. Behind the Monument, the service had a flavour of damaged oranges, which, a little further down towards the river, tempered into herrings, and gradually toned into a cosmopolitan blast of fish. In one church, the exact counterpart of the church in the Rake's Progress where the hero is being married to the horrible old lady, there was no speciality of atmosphere, until the organ shook a perfume of hides all over us from some adjacent warehouse.

Be the scent what it would, however, there was no speciality in the people. There were never enough of them to represent any calling or neighbourhood. They had all gone elsewhere over-night, and the few stragglers in the many churches languished there inexpressively.

Among the uncommercial travels in which I have engaged, this year of Sunday travel occupies its own place, apart from all the rest. Whether I think of the church where the sails of the oyster-boats in the river almost flapped against the windows, or of the church where the railroad made the bells hum as the train rushed by above the roof, I recal a curious experience. On summer Sundays, in the gentle rain or the bright sunshine—either, deepening the idleness of the idle City—I have sat, in that singular silence which belongs to resting-places usually astir, in scores of buildings at the heart of the world's metropolis, unknown to far greater numbers of people speaking the English tongue, than the ancient edifices of the Eternal City, or the Pyramids of Egypt. The dark vestries and registries into which I have peeped, and the little hemmed-in churchyards that have echoed to my feet, have left impressions on my memory as distinct and quaint as any it has in that way received. In all those dusty registers that the worms are eating, there is not a line but made some hearts leap, or some tears flow, in their day. Still and dry now, still and dry! and the old tree at the window with no room for its branches, has seen them all out. So with the tomb of the old Master of the old Company, on which it drips. His son restored it and died, his daughter restored it and died, and then he had been remembered long enough, and the tree took possession of him, and his name cracked out.

There are few more striking indications of the changes of manners and customs that two or three hundred years have brought about, than these deserted Churches. Many of them are handsome and costly structures, several of them were designed by WREN, many of them arose from the ashes of the great fire, others of them outlived the plague and the fire too, to die a slow death in these later days. No one can be sure of the coming time; but it is not too much to say of it that it has no sign in its outsetting tides, of the reflux to these churches of their congregations and uses. They remain like the tombs of the old citizens who lie beneath them and around them, Monuments of another age. They are worth a Sunday-exploration now and then, for they yet echo, not unharmoniously, to the time when the city of London really was London; when the 'Prentices and Trained Bands were of mark in the state; when even the Lord Mayor himself was a Reality—not a Fiction conventionally be-puffed on one day in the year by illustrious friends, who no less conventionally laugh at him on the remaining three hundred and sixty-four days.

X.

SHY NEIGHBOURHOODS.

So much of my travelling is done on foot, that if I cherished betting propensities, I should probably be found registered in sporting newspapers, under some such title as the Elastic Novice, challenging all eleven-stone mankind to competition in walking. My last special feat was turning out of bed at two, after a hard day, pedestrian and otherwise, and walking thirty miles into the country to breakfast. The road was so lonely in the night, that I fell asleep to the monotonous sound of my own feet, doing their regular four miles an hour. Mile after mile I walked, without the slightest sense of exertion, dozing heavily and dreaming constantly. It was only when I made a stumble like a drunken man, or struck out into the road to avoid a horseman close upon me on the path —who had no existence—that I came to myself and looked about. The day broke mistily (it was autumn time), and I could not disembarrass myself of the idea that I had to climb those heights and banks of cloud, and that there was an Alpine Convent somewhere behind the sun, where I was going to breakfast. This sleepy notion was so much stronger than such substantial objects as villages and haystacks, that, after the sun was up and bright, and when I was sufficiently awake to have a sense of pleasure in the prospect, I still occasionally caught myself looking about for wooden arms to point the right track up the mountain, and wondering there was no snow yet. It is a curiosity of broken sleep, that I made immense quantities of verses on that pedestrian occasion (of course I never make any when I am in my right senses), and that I spoke a certain language once pretty familiar to me, but which I have nearly forgotten from disuse, with fluency. Of both these phenomena I have such frequent experience in the state between sleeping and waking, that I sometimes argue with myself that I know I cannot be awake, for, if I were, I should not be half so ready. The readiness is not imaginary, because I often recal long strings of the verses, and many turns of the fluent speech, after I am broad awake.

My walking is of two kinds: one, straight on end to a definite goal at a round pace; one, objectless, loitering, and purely vagabond. In the latter state, no gipsy on earth is a greater vagabond than myself; it is so natural to me and strong with me, that I think I must be the descendant, at no great distance, of some irreclaimable tramp.

One of the pleasantest things I have lately met with, in a vagabond course of shy metropolitan neighbourhoods and small shops, is the fancy of a humble artist as exemplified in two portraits representing Mr. Thomas Sayers, of Great Britain, and Mr. John Heenan, of the United States of America. These illustrious men are highly coloured, in fighting trim, and fighting attitude. To suggest the pastoral and meditative nature of their peaceful calling, Mr. Heenan is represented on emerald sward, with primroses and other modest flowers springing up under the heels of his half-boots; while Mr. Sayers is impelled to the administration of his favourite blow, the Auctioneer, by the silent eloquence of a village church. The humble homes of England, with their domestic virtues and honeysuckle porches, urge both heroes to go in and win; and the lark and other singing-birds are observable in the upper air, ecstatically carolling their thanks to Heaven for a fight. On the whole, the associations entwined with the pugilistic art by this artist are much in the manner of Izaak Walton.

But, it is with the lower animals of back streets and by-ways that my present purpose rests. For human notes we may return to such neighbourhoods when leisure and opportunity serve.

Nothing in shy neighbourhoods perplexes my mind more, than the bad company birds keep. Foreign birds often get into good society, but British birds are inseparable from low associates. There is a whole street of them in Saint Giles's; and I always find them in poor and immoral neighbourhoods, convenient to the public-house and the pawnbroker's. They seem to lead people into drinking, and even the man who makes their cages usually gets into a chronic state of black eye. Why is this? Also, they will do things for people in short-skirted velveteen coats with bone buttons, or in sleeved waistcoats and fur caps, which they cannot be persuaded by the respectable orders of society to undertake. In a dirty court in Spitalfields, once, I found a goldfinch drawing his own water, and drawing as much of it as if he were in a consuming fever. That goldfinch lived at a bird-shop, and offered, in writing, to barter himself against old clothes, empty bottles, or even kitchen-stuff. Surely a low thing and a depraved taste in any finch! I bought that goldfinch for money. He was sent home, and hung upon a nail over against my table. He lived outside a counterfeit dwelling-house, supposed (as I argued) to be a dyer's; otherwise it would have been impossible to account for his perch sticking out of the garret window. From the time of his appearance in my room, either he left off being thirsty—which was not in the bond—or he could not make up his mind to hear his little bucket drop back into his well when he let it go : a shock which in the best of times had made him tremble. He drew no water but by stealth and under the cloak of night. After an interval of futile and at length hopeless expectation, the merchant who had educated him was appealed to. The merchant was a bow-legged character, with a flat and cushiony nose, like the last new strawberry. He wore a fur cap, and shorts, and was of the velveteen race, velveteeny. He sent word that he would "look round." He looked round, appeared in the doorway of the room, and slightly cocked up his evil eye at the goldfinch. Instantly a raging thirst beset that bird; when it was appeased, he still drew several unnecessary buckets of water;

and finally, leaped about his perch and sharpened his bill, as if he had been to the nearest wine-vaults and got drunk.

Donkeys again. I know shy neighbourhoods where the Donkey goes in at the street door, and appears to live up-stairs, for I have examined the back-yard from over the palings, and have been unable to make him out. Gentility, nobility, Royalty, would appeal to that donkey in vain to do what he does for a costermonger. Feed him with oats at the highest price, put an infant prince and princess in a pair of panniers on his back, adjust his delicate trappings to a nicety, take him to the softest slopes at Windsor, and try what pace you can get out of him. Then, starve him, harness him anyhow to a truck with a flat tray on it, and see him bowl from Whitechapel to Bayswater. There appears to be no particular private understanding between birds and donkeys, in a state of nature; but in the shy neighbourhood state, you shall see them always in the same hands, and always developing their very best energies for the very worst company. I have known a donkey—by sight; we were not on speaking terms—who lived over on the Surrey side of London-bridge, among the fastnesses of Jacob's Island and Dockhead. It was the habit of that animal, when his services were not in immediate requisition, to go out alone, idling. I have met him, a mile from his place of residence, loitering about the streets; and the expression of his countenance at such times was most degraded. He was attached to the establishment of an elderly lady who sold periwinkles, and he used to stand on Saturday nights with a cartful of those delicacies outside a gin-shop, pricking up his ears when a customer came to the cart, and too evidently deriving satisfaction from the knowledge that they got bad measure. His mistress was sometimes overtaken by inebriety. The last time I ever saw him (about five years ago) he was in circumstances of difficulty, caused by this failing. Having been left alone with the cart of periwinkles, and forgotten, he went off idling. He prowled among his usual low haunts for some time, gratifying his depraved tastes, until, not taking the cart into his calculations, he endeavoured to turn up a narrow alley, and became greatly involved. He was taken into custody by the police, and, the Green Yard of the district being near at hand, was backed into that place of durance. At that crisis, I encountered him; the stubborn sense he evinced of being—not to compromise the expression—a blackguard, I never saw exceeded in the human subject. A flaring candle in a paper shade, stuck in among his periwinkles, showed him, with his ragged harness broken and his cart extensively shattered, twitching his mouth and shaking his hanging head, a picture of disgrace and obduracy. I have seen boys being taken to station-houses, who were as like him as his own brother. .

The dogs of shy neighbourhoods, I observe to avoid play, and to be conscious of poverty. They avoid work too, if they can, of course; that is in the nature of all animals. I have the pleasure to know a dog in a back street in the neighbourhood of Walworth, who has greatly distinguished himself in the minor drama, and who takes his portrait with him when he makes an engagement, for the illustration of the play-bill. His portrait (which is not at all like him) represents him in the act of dragging to the earth a recreant Indian, who is supposed to have tomahawked, or essayed to tomahawk, a British officer. The design is pure poetry, for there is no such Indian in the piece, and no such incident. He is a dog of the Newfoundland breed, for whose honesty I would be bail to any amount; but whose intellectual qualities in association with dramatic fiction, I cannot rate high. Indeed, he is too honest for the profession he has entered. Being at a town in Yorkshire last summer, and seeing him posted in the bill of the night, I attended the performance. His first scene was eminently successful; but, as it occupied a second in its representation (and five lines in the bill), it scarcely afforded ground for a cool and deliberate judgment of his powers. He had merely to bark, run on, and jump through an inn window after a comic fugitive. The next scene of importance to the fable was a little marred in its interest by his over-anxiety: forasmuch as while his master (a belated soldier in a den of robbers on a tempestuous night) was feelingly lamenting the absence of his faithful dog, and laying great stress on the fact that he was thirty leagues away, the faithful dog was barking furiously in the prompter's box, and clearly choking himself against his collar. But it was in his greatest scene of all, that his honesty got the better of him. He had to enter a dense and trackless forest, on the trail of the murderer, and there to fly at the murderer when he found him resting at the foot of a tree, with his victim bound ready for slaughter. It was a hot night, and he came into the forest from an altogether unexpected direction, in the sweetest temper, at a very deliberate trot, not in the least excited; trotted to the foot-lights with his tongue out; and there sat down, panting, and amiably surveying the audience, with his tail beating on the boards, like a Dutch clock. Meanwhile the murderer, impatient to receive his doom, was audibly calling to him "Co-o-ome here!" while the victim, struggling with his bonds, assailed him with the most injurious expressions. It happened through these means, that when he was in course of time persuaded to trot up and rend the murderer limb from limb, he made it (for dramatic purposes) a little too obvious that he worked out that awful retribution by licking butter off his blood-stained hands.

In a shy street, behind Long-acre, two honest dogs live, who perform in Punch's shows. I may venture to say that I am on terms of intimacy with both, and that I never saw either guilty of the falsehood of failing to look down at the man inside the show, during the whole performance. The difficulty other dogs have in satisfying their minds about these dogs, appears to be never overcome by time. The same dogs must encounter them over and over again, as they trudge along in their off-minutes behind the legs of the show and beside the drum; but all dogs seem to suspect their frills and jackets, and to sniff at them as if they thought those articles of personal adornment, an eruption—a something in the nature of mange, perhaps. From this Covent-garden window of mine I noticed a country dog, only the other day, who had come up to Covent-garden Market under a cart, and had broken his cord, an end of which he still trailed along with him. He loitered about the corners of the four streets commanded by my window; and bad London dogs came up, and told him lies that he didn't believe; and worse London dogs came up, and made proposals to him to go and steal in the market, which his principles rejected; and the ways of the town confused him, and he crept aside and lay down in a doorway. He had scarcely got a wink of sleep, when up comes Punch with Toby. He was darting to Toby for consolation and advice, when he saw the frill, and stopped in the middle of the street, appalled. The show was pitched, Toby retired behind the drapery, the audience formed, the drum and pipes struck up. My country dog remained immovable, intently staring at these strange appearances, until Toby opened the drama by appearing on his ledge, and to him entered Punch, who put a tobacco-pipe into Toby's mouth. At this spectacle, the country dog threw up his head, gave one terrible howl, and fled due west.

We talk of men keeping dogs, but we might often talk more expressively of dogs keeping men. I know a bulldog in a shy corner of Hammersmith who keeps a man. He keeps him up a yard, and makes him go to public-houses and lay wagers on him, and obliges him to lean against posts and look at him, and forces him to neglect work for him, and keeps him under rigid coercion. I once knew a fancy terrier who kept a gentleman—a gentleman who had been brought up at Oxford, too. The dog kept the gentleman entirely for his glorification, and the gentleman never talked about anything but the terrier. This, however, was not in a shy neighbourhood, and is a digression consequently.

There are a great many dogs in shy neighbourhoods, who keep boys. I have my eye on a mongrel in Somerstown who keeps three boys. He feigns that he can bring down sparrows, and unburrow rats (he can do neither), and he takes the boys out on sporting pretences into all sorts of suburban fields. He has likewise made them believe that he possesses some mysterious knowledge of the art of fishing, and they consider themselves incompletely equipped for the Hampstead ponds, with a pickle-jar and a wide-mouthed bottle, unless he is with them and barking tremendously. There is a dog residing in the Borough of Southwark who keeps a blind man. He may be seen, most days, in Oxford-street, haling the blind man away on expeditions wholly uncontemplated by, and unintelligible to, the man : wholly of the dog's conception and execution. Contrariwise, when the man has projects, the dog will sit down in a crowded thoroughfare and meditate. I saw him yesterday, wearing the money-tray like an easy collar, instead of offering it to the public, taking the man against his will, on the invitation of a disreputable cur, apparently to visit a dog at Harrow—he was so intent on that direction. The north wall of Burlington House Gardens, between the Arcade and the Albany, offers a shy spot for appointments among blind men at about two or three o'clock in the afternoon. They sit (very uncomfortably) on a sloping stone there, and compare notes. Their dogs may always be observed at the same time, openly disparaging the men they keep, to one another, and settling where they shall respectively take their men when they begin to move again. At a small butcher's, in a shy neighbourhood (there is no reason for suppressing the name; it is by Notting-hill, and gives upon the district called the Potteries), I know a shaggy black and white dog who keeps a drover. He is a dog of an easy disposition, and too frequently allows this drover to get drunk. On these occasions, it is the dog's custom to sit outside the public-house, keeping his eye on a few sheep, and thinking. I have seen him with six sheep, plainly casting up in his mind how many he began with when he left the market, and at what places he has left the rest. I have seen him perplexed by not being able to account to himself for certain particular sheep. A light has gradually broken on him, he has remembered at what butcher's he left them, and in a burst of grave satisfaction has caught a fly off his nose, and shown himself much relieved. If I could at any time have doubted the fact that it was he who kept the drover, and not the drover who kept him, it would have been abundantly proved by his way of taking undivided charge of the six sheep, when the drover came out besmeared with red ochre and beer, and gave him wrong directions, which he calmly disregarded. He has taken the sheep entirely into his own hands, has merely remarked with respectful firmness, "That instruction would place them under an omnibus;

you had better confine your attention to yourself—you will want it all;" and has driven his charge away, with an intelligence of ears and tail, and a knowledge of business, that has left his lout of a man very, very far behind.

As the dogs of shy neighbourhoods usually betray a slinking consciousness of being in poor circumstances—for the most part manifested in an aspect of anxiety, an awkwardness in their play, and a misgiving that somebody is going to harness them to something, to pick up a living—so the cats of shy neighbourhoods exhibit a strong tendency to relapse into barbarism. Not only are they made selfishly ferocious by ruminating on the surplus population around them, and on the densely crowded state of all the avenues to cat's meat; not only is there a moral and politico-economical haggardness in them, traceable to these reflections; but they evince a physical deterioration. Their linen is not clean, and is wretchedly got up; their black turns rusty, like old mourning; they wear very indifferent fur; and take to the shabbiest cotton velvet, instead of silk velvet. I am on terms of recognition with several small streets of cats, about the Obelisk in Saint George's Fields, and also in the vicinity of Clerkenwell-green, and also in the back settlements of Drury-lane. In appearance, they are very like the women among whom they live. They seem to turn out of their unwholesome beds into the street, without any preparation. They leave their young families to stagger about the gutters, unassisted, while they frouzily quarrel and swear and scratch and spit, at street corners. In particular, I remark that when they are about to increase their families (an event of frequent recurrence) the resemblance is strongly expressed in a certain dusty dowdiness, down-at-heel self-neglect, and general giving up of things. I cannot honestly report that I have ever seen a feline matron of this class washing her face when in an interesting condition.

Not to prolong these notes of uncommercial travel among the lower animals of shy neighbourhoods, by dwelling at length upon the exasperated moodiness of the tom-cats, and their resemblance in many respects to a man and a brother, I will come to a close with a word on the fowls of the same localities.

That anything born of an egg and invested with wings, should have got to the pass that it hops contentedly down a ladder into a cellar, and calls *that* going home, is a circumstance so amazing as to leave one nothing more in this connexion to wonder at. Otherwise I might wonder at the completeness with which these fowls have become separated from all the birds of the air—have taken to grovelling in bricks and mortar and mud—have forgotten all about live trees, and make roosting-places of shop-boards, barrows, oyster-tubs, bulk-heads, and door-scrapers. I wonder at nothing concerning them, and take them as they are. I accept as products of Nature and things of course, a reduced Bantam family of my acquaintance in the Hackney-road, who are incessantly at the pawnbroker's. I cannot say that they enjoy themselves, for they are of a melancholy temperament; but what enjoyment they are capable of, they derive from crowding together in the pawnbroker's side-entry. Here, they are always to be found in a feeble flutter, as if they were newly come down in the world, and were afraid of being identified. I know a low fellow, originally of a good family from Dorking, who takes his whole establishment of wives, in single file, in at the door of the Jug Department of a disorderly tavern near the Haymarket, manœuvres them among the company's legs, emerges with them at the Bottle Entrance, and so passes his life: seldom, in the season, going to bed before two in the morning. Over Waterloo-bridge, there is a shabby old speckled couple (they belong to the wooden French-bedstead, washing-stand, and towel-horse-making trade), who are always trying to get in at the door of a chapel. Whether the old lady, under a delusion reminding one of Mrs. Southcott, has an idea of entrusting an egg to that particular denomination, or merely understands that she has no business in the building and is consequently frantic to enter it, I cannot determine; but she is constantly endeavouring to undermine the principal door: while her partner, who is infirm upon his legs, walks up and down, encouraging her and defying the Universe. But, the family I have been best acquainted with, since the removal from this trying sphere of a Chinese circle at Brentford, reside in the densest part of Bethnal-green. Their abstraction from the objects among which they live, or rather their conviction that those objects have all come into existence in express subservience to fowls, has so enchanted me, that I have made them the subject of many journeys at divers hours. After careful observation of the two lords and the ten ladies of whom this family consists, I have come to the conclusion that their opinions are represented by the leading lord and leading lady: the latter, as I judge, an aged personage, afflicted with a paucity of feather and visibility of quill, that gives her the appearance of a bundle of office pens. When a railway goods-van that would crush an elephant comes round the corner, tearing over these fowls, they emerge unharmed from under the horses, perfectly satisfied that the whole rush was a passing property in the air, which may have left something to eat behind it. They look upon old shoes, wrecks of kettles and saucepans, and fragments of bonnets, as a kind of meteoric discharge, for fowls to peck at. Peg-tops and hoops they account, I think, as a sort of hail; shuttlecocks, as rain, or dew. Gaslight comes quite as natural to them as any other light; and I have more than a suspicion that, in the minds of the two lords, the early public-house at the corner has superseded the sun. I have established it as a certain fact, that they always begin to crow when the public-house shutters begin to be taken down, and that they salute the potboy, the instant he appears to perform that duty, as if he were Phœbus in person.

XI.

TRAMPS.

The chance use of the word "Tramp" in my last paper, brought that numerous fraternity so vividly before my mind's eye, that I had no sooner laid down my pen than a compulsion was upon me to take it up again, and make notes of the Tramps whom I perceived on all the summer roads in all directions.

Whenever a tramp sits down to rest by the wayside, he sits with his legs in a dry ditch; and whenever he goes to sleep (which is very often indeed), he goes to sleep on his back. Yonder, by the high road, glaring white in the bright sunshine, lies, on the dusty bit of turf under the bramble-bush that fences the coppice from the highway, the tramp of the order savage, fast asleep. He lies on the broad of his back, with his face turned up to the sky, and one of his ragged arms loosely thrown across his face. His bundle (what can be the contents of that mysterious bundle, to make it worth his while to carry it about?) is thrown down beside him, and the waking woman with him sits with her legs in the ditch, and her back to the road. She wears her bonnet rakishly perched on the front of her head, to shade her face from the sun in walking, and she ties her skirts round her in conventionally tight tramp-fashion with a sort of apron. You can seldom catch sight of her, resting thus, without seeing her in a despondently defiant manner doing something to her hair or her bonnet, and glancing at you between her fingers. She does not often go to sleep herself in the daytime, but will sit for any length of time beside the man. And his slumberous propensities would not seem to be referable to the fatigue of carrying the bundle, for she carries it much oftener and further than he. When they are afoot, you will mostly find him slouching on ahead, in a gruff temper, while she lags heavily behind with the burden. He is given to personally correcting her, too—which phase of his character develops itself oftenest, on benches outside alehouse doors—and she appears to become strongly attached to him for these reasons; it may usually be noticed that when the poor creature has a bruised face, she is the most affectionate. He has no occupation whatever, this order of tramp, and has no object whatever in going anywhere. He will sometimes call himself a brickmaker, or a sawyer, but only when he takes an imaginative flight. He generally represents himself, in a vague way, as looking out for a job of work; but he never did work, he never does, and he never never will. It is a favourite fiction with him, however (as if he were the most industrious character on earth), that *you* never work; and as he goes past your garden and sees you looking at your flowers, you will overhear him growl, with a strong sense of contrast, "*You* are a lucky hidle devil, *you* are!"

The slinking tramp is of the same hopeless order, and has the same injured conviction on him that you were born to whatever you possess, and never did anything to get it; but he is of a less audacious disposition. He will stop before your gate, and say to his female companion with an air of constitutional humility and propitiation— to edify any one who may be within hearing behind a blind or a bush—"This is a sweet spot, ain't it? A lovelly spot! And I wonder if they'd give two poor footsore travellers like me and you, a drop of fresh water out of such a pretty gen-teel crib? We'd take it wery koind on 'em, wouldn't us? Wery koind, upon my word, us would!" He has a quick sense of a dog in the vicinity, and will extend his modestly-injured propitiation to the dog chained up in your yard: remarking, as he slinks at the yard gate, "Ah! You are a foine breed o' dog, too, and *you* ain't kep for nothink! I'd take it wery koind o' your master if he'd elp a traveller and his woife as envies no gentlefolk their good fortun, wi' a bit o' your broken wittles. He'd never know the want of it, nor more would you. Don't bark like that, at poor persons as never done you no arm; the poor is down-trodden and broke enough without that; O DON'T!" He generally heaves a prodigious sigh in moving away, and always looks up the lane and down the lane, and up the road and down the road, before going on.

Both of these orders of tramp are of a very robust habit; let the hard-working labourer at whose cottage-door they prowl and beg, have the ague never so badly, these tramps are sure to be in good health.

There is another kind of tramp, whom you encounter this bright summer day—say, on a road with the sea-breeze making its dust lively, and sails of ships in the blue distance beyond the slope of Down. As you walk enjoyingly on, you descry in the perspective at the bottom of a steep hill up which your way lies, a figure that appears to be sitting airily on a gate, whistling in a cheerful and disengaged manner. As you approach nearer to it, you observe the figure to slide down from the gate, to desist from whistling, to uncock its hat, to become tender of foot, to depress its head and elevate its shoulders, and to present all the characteristics of profound despondency. Arriving at the bottom of the hill and coming close to the figure, you observe it to be the figure of a shabby young man. He is moving painfully forward, in the direction in which you are going, and his mind is so preoccupied with his misfortunes that he is not aware of your approach until you are close upon him at the hill-foot. When he is aware of you, you discover him to be a remarkably well-behaved young man, and a remarkably well-spoken young man. You know him to be well-behaved, by his respectful manner of touching his hat; you know him to be well-spoken, by his smooth manner of expressing himself. He says in a flowing confidential voice, and without punctuation, "I ask your pardon sir but if you would excuse the liberty of being so addressed upon the public Iway by one who is almost reduced to rags though it as not always been so and by no fault of his own but through ill elth in his family and many unmerited sufferings it would be a great obligation sir to know the time." You give the well-spoken young man, the time. The well-spoken young man, keeping well up with you, resumes: "I am aware sir that it is a liberty to intrude a further question on a gentleman walking for his entertainment but might I make so bold as ask the favour of the way to Dover sir and about the distance?" You inform the well-spoken young man that the way to Dover is straight on, and the distance some eighteen miles. The well-spoken young man becomes greatly agitated. "In the condition to which I am reduced," says he, "I could not ope to reach Dover before dark even if my shoes were in a state to take me there or my feet were in a state to old out over the flinty road and were not on the bare ground of which any gentleman has the means to satisfy himself by looking Sir may I take the liberty of speaking to you?" As the well-spoken young man keeps so well up with you that you can't prevent his taking the liberty of speaking to you, he goes on, with fluency: "Sir it is not begging that is my intention for I was brought up by the best of mothers and begging is not my trade I should not know sir how to follow it as a trade if such were my shameful wishes for the best of mothers long taught otherwise and in the best of omes though now reduced to take the present liberty on the Iway Sir my business was the law-stationering and I was favourably known to the Solicitor-General the Attorney-General the majority of the Judges and the ole of the legal profession but through ill elth in my family and the treachery of a friend for whom I became security and he no other than my own wife's brother the brother of my own wife I was cast forth with my tender partner and three young children not to beg for I will sooner die of deprivation but to make my way to the seaport town of Dover where I have a relative i in respect not only that will assist me but that would trust me with untold gold Sir in appier times and hare this calamity fell upon me I made for my amusement when I little thought that I should ever need it excepting for my air this"—here the well-spoken young man puts his hand into his breast—" this comb! Sir I implore you in the name of charity to purchase a tortoiseshell comb which is a genuine article at any price that your humanity may put upon it and may the blessings of a ouseless family awaiting with beating arts the return of a husband and a father from Dover upon the cold stone seats of London-bridge ever attend you Sir may I take the liberty of speaking to you I implore you to buy this comb!" By this time, being a reasonably good walker, you will have been too much for the well-spoken young man, who will stop short and express his disgust and his want of breath, in a long expectoration, as you leave him behind.

Towards the end of the same walk, on the same bright summer day, at the corner of the next little town or village, you may find another kind of tramp, embodied in the persons of a most exemplary couple whose only improvidence appears to have been, that they spent the last of their little All on soap. They are a man and woman, spotless to behold—John Anderson, with the frost on his short smock-frock instead of his "pow," attended by Mrs. Anderson. John is over-ostentatious of the frost upon his raiment, and wears a curious and, you would say, an almost unnecessary demonstration of girdle of white linen wound about his waist—a girdle, snowy as Mrs. Anderson's apron. This cleanliness was the expiring effort of the respectable couple, and nothing then remained to Mr. Anderson but to get chalked upon his spade in snow-white copy-book characters, HUNGRY! and to sit down here. Yes; one thing more remained to Mr. Anderson—his character; Monarchs could not deprive him of his hard-earned character. Accordingly, as you come up with this spectacle of virtue in distress, Mrs. Anderson rises, and with a decent curtsey presents for your consideration a certificate from a Doctor of Divinity, the reverend the Vicar of Upper Dodgington, who informs his Christian friends and all whom it may concern that the bearers, John Anderson and lawful wife, are persons to whom you cannot be too liberal. This benevolent pastor omitted no work of his hands to fit the good couple out, for with half an eye you can recognise his autograph on the spade.

Another class of tramp is a man, the most valuable part of whose stock-in-trade is a highly perplexed demeanour. He is got up like a countryman, and you will often come upon the poor fellow, while he is endeavouring to decipher the inscription on a milestone—quite a fruitless endeavour, for he cannot read. He asks your pardon, he truly does (he is very slow of speech, this tramp, and he looks in a bewildered way all round the prospect while he talks to you), but all of us shold do as we wold be done by, and he'll take it kind, if you'll put a power man in the right road fur to jine his eldest son as has broke his leg bad in the masoning, and is in this heere Orspit'l as is wrote down by Squire Pouncerby's own hand as wold not tell a lie fur no man. He then produces from under his dark frock (being always very slow and perplexed) a neat but worn old leathern purse, from which he takes a scrap of paper. On this scrap of paper is written, by Squire Pouncerby, of The Grove, "Please to direct the Bearer, a poor but very worthy man, to the Sussex County Hospital, near Brighton"—a matter of some difficulty at the moment, seeing that the request comes suddenly upon you in the depths of Hertfordshire. The more you endeavour to indicate where Brighton is—when you have with the greatest difficulty remembered—the less the devoted father can be made to comprehend, and the more obtusely he stares at the prospect; whereby, being reduced to extremity, you recommend the faithful parent to begin by going to St. Albans, and present him with half-a-crown. It does him good, no doubt, but scarcely helps him forward, since you find him lying drunk that same evening in the wheelwright's sawpit under the shed where the felled trees are, opposite the sign of the Three Jolly Hedgers.

But, the most vicious, by far, of all the idle tramps, is the tramp who pretends to have been a gentleman. "Educated," he writes, from the village beer-shop in pale ink of a ferruginous complexion; "educated at Trin. Coll. Cam.—nursed in the lap of affluence—once in my small way the pattron of the Muses," &c. &c. &c. —surely a sympathetic mind will not withhold a trifle, to help him on to the market-town where he thinks of giving a Lecture to the *fruges consumere nati*, on things in general? This shameful creature lolling about hedge taprooms in his ragged clothes, now so far from being black that they look as if they never can have been black, is more selfish and insolent than even the savage tramp. He would sponge on the poorest boy for a farthing, and spurn him when he had got it; he would interpose (if he could get anything by it) between the baby and the mother's breast. So much lower than the company he keeps, for his maudlin assumption of being higher, this pitiless rascal blights the summer road as he maunders on between the luxuriant hedges: where (to my thinking) even the wild convolvulus and rose and sweetbriar, are the worse for his going by, and need time to recover from the taint of him in the air.

The young fellows who trudge along barefoot, five or six together, their boots slung over their shoulders, their shabby bundles under their arms, their sticks newly cut from some roadside wood, are not eminently prepossessing, but are much less objectionable. There is a tramp-fellowship among them. They pick one another up at resting stations, and go on in companies. They always go at a fast swing—though they generally limp too—and there is invariably one of the company who has much ado to keep up with the rest. They generally talk about horses, and any other means of locomotion than walking: or, one of the company relates some recent experiences of the road—which are always disputes and difficulties. As for example. "So as I'm a standing at the pump in the market, blest if there don't come up a Beadle, and he ses, 'Mustn't stand here,' he ses. 'Why not?' I ses. 'No beggars allowed in this town,' he ses. 'Who's a beggar?' I ses. 'You are,' he ses. 'Who ever see *me* beg? Did *you*?' I ses. 'Then you're a tramp,' he ses. 'I'd rather be that, than a Beadle,' I ses." (The company express great approval.) "'Would you,' he ses to me. 'Yes I would,' I ses to him. 'Well,' he ses, 'anyhow, get out of this town.' 'Why, blow your little town!' I ses, 'who wants to be in it? Wot does your dirty little town mean by comin' and stickin' itself in the road to anywhere? Why don't you get a shovel and a barrer, and clear your town out o' people's way?'" (The company expressing the highest approval and laughing aloud, they all go down the hill.)

Then, there are the tramp handicraft men. Are they not all over England, in this Midsummer time? Where does the lark sing, the corn grow, the mill turn, the river run, and they are not among the lights and shadows, tinkering, chair-mending, umbrella-mending, clock-mending, knife-grinding? Surely, a pleasant thing, if we were in that condition of life, to grind our way through Kent, Sussex, and Surrey. For the first six weeks or so, we should see the sparks we ground off, fiery bright against a background of green wheat and green leaves. A little later, and the ripe harvest would pale our sparks from red to yellow, until we got the dark newly-turned land for a background again, and they were red once more.

By that time, we should have ground our way to the sea cliffs, and the whirr of our wheel would be lost in the breaking of the waves. Our next variety in sparks would be derived from contrast with the gorgeous medley of colours in the autumn woods, and, by the time we had ground our way round to the heathy lands between Reigate and Croydon, doing a prosperous stroke of business all along, we should show like a little firework in the light frosty air, and be the next best thing to the blacksmith's forge. Very agreeable, too, to go on a chair-mending tour. What judges we should be of rushes, and how knowingly (with a sheaf and a bottomless chair at our back) we should lounge on bridges, looking over at osier-beds. Among all the innumerable occupations that cannot possibly be transacted without the assistance of lookers-on, chair-mending may take a station in the first rank. When we sat down with our backs against the barn or the public-house, and began to mend, what a sense of popularity would grow upon us. When all the children came to look at us, and the tailor, and the general dealer, and the farmer who had been giving a small order at the little saddler's, and the groom from the great house, and the publican, and even the two skittle-players (and here note that, howsoever busy all the rest of village human-kind may be, there will always be two people with leisure to play at skittles, wherever village skittles are), what encouragement would be on us to plait and weave! No one looks at us while we plait and weave these words. Clock-mending again. Except for the slight inconvenience of carrying a clock under our arm, and the monotony of making the bell go, whenever we came to a human habitation, what a pleasant privilege to give a voice to the dumb cottage-clock, and set it talking to the cottage family again. Likewise we foresee great interest in going round by the park plantations, under the overhanging boughs (hares, rabbits, partridges, and pheasants, scudding like mad across and across the chequered ground before us), and so over the park ladder, and through the wood, until we came to the Keeper's lodge. Then, would the Keeper be discoverable at his door, in a deep nest of leaves, smoking his pipe. Then, on our accosting him in the way of our trade, would he call to Mrs. Keeper, respecting "t'ould clock" in the kitchen. Then, would Mrs. Keeper ask us into the lodge, and on due examination we should offer to make a good job of it for eighteenpence: which offer, being accepted, would set us tinkling and clinking among the chubby awe-struck little Keepers for an hour and more. So completely to the family's satisfaction would we achieve our work, that the Keeper would mention how that there was something wrong with the bell of the turret stable-clock up at the Hall, and that if we thought good of going up to the housekeeper on the chance of that job too, why he would take us. Then, should we go, among the branching oaks and the deep fern, by silent ways of mystery known to the Keeper, seeing the herd glancing here and there as we went along, until we came to the old Hall, solemn and grand. Under the Terrace Flower Garden, and round by the stables, would the Keeper take us in, and as we passed we should observe how spacious and stately the stables, and how fine the painting of the horses' names over their stalls, and how solitary all: the family being in London. Then, should we find ourselves presented to the housekeeper, sitting, in hushed state, at needlework, in a bay-window looking out upon a mighty grim red-brick quadrangle, guarded by stone lions disrespectfully throwing somersaults over the escutcheons of the noble family. Then, our services accepted and we insinuated with a candle into the stable-turret, we should find it to be a mere question of pendulum, but one that would hold us until dark. Then, should we fall to work, with a general impression of Ghosts being about, and of pictures indoors that of a certainty came out of their frames and "walked," if the family would only own it. Then, should we work and work, until the day gradually turned to dusk, and even until the dusk gradually turned to dark. Our task at length accomplished, we should be taken into an enormous servants' hall, and there regaled with beef and bread, and powerful ale. Then, paid freely, we should be at liberty to go, and should be told by a pointing helper to keep round over yinder by the blasted ash, and so straight through the woods, till we should see the town-lights right afore us. Then, feeling lonesome, should we desire upon the whole, that the ash had not been blasted, or that the helper had had the manners not to mention it. However, we should keep on, all right, till suddenly the stable bell would strike ten in the dolefullest way, quite chilling our blood, though we had so lately taught him how to acquit himself. Then, as we went on, should we recal old stories, and dimly consider what it would be most advisable to do, in the event of a tall figure, all in white, with saucer eyes, coming up and saying, "I want you to come to a churchyard and mend a church clock. Follow me!" Then, should we make a burst to get clear of the trees, and should soon find ourselves in the open, with the town-lights bright ahead of us. So should we lie that night at the ancient sign of the Crispin and Crispanus, and rise early next morning to be betimes on tramp again.

Bricklayers often tramp, in twos and threes, lying by night at their "lodges" which are scattered all over the country. Bricklaying is another of the occupations that can by no means be transacted in rural parts, without the assistance of spectators—of as many as can be convened. In thinly-peopled spots, I have known bricklayers on tramp, coming up with bricklayers at work, to be so sensible of the indispensability of lookers-on, that they themselves have set up in that capacity, and have been unable to subside into the acceptance of a proffered share in the job, for two or three days together. Sometimes, the "navvy," on tramp, with an extra pair of half-boots over his shoulder, a bag, a bottle, and a can, will take a similar part in a job of excavation, and will look at it without engaging in it, until all his money is gone. The current of my uncommercial pursuits caused me only last summer to want a little body of workmen for a certain spell of work in a pleasant part of the country; and I was at one time honoured with the attendance of as many as seven-and-twenty, who were looking at six.

Who can be familiar with any rustic highway in the summer-time, without storing up knowledge of the many tramps who go from one oasis of town or village to another, to sell a stock in trade, apparently not worth a shilling when sold? Shrimps are a favourite commodity for this kind of speculation, and so are cakes of a soft and spongy character, coupled with Spanish nuts and brandy balls. The stock is carried on the head in a basket, and, between the head and the basket, are the trestles on which the stock is displayed at trading times. Fleet of foot, but a careworn class of tramp this, mostly; with a certain stiffness of neck, occasioned by much anxious balancing of baskets; and also with a long Chinese sort of eye, which an overweighted forehead would seem to have squeezed into that form.

On the hot dusty roads near seaport towns and great rivers, behold the tramping Soldier. And if you should happen never to have asked yourself whether his uniform is suited to his work, perhaps the poor fellow's appearance as he comes distressfully towards you, with his absurdly tight jacket unbuttoned, his neck-gear in his hand, and his legs well chafed by his trousers of baize, may suggest the personal inquiry, how you think *you* would like it. Much better the tramping Sailor, although his cloth is somewhat too thick for land service. But, why the tramping merchant-mate should put on a black velvet waistcoat, for a chalky country in the dog-days, is one of the great secrets of nature that will never be discovered.

I have my eye upon a piece of Kentish road, bordered on either side by a wood, and having on one hand, between the road-dust and the trees, a skirting patch of grass. Wild flowers grow in abundance on this spot, and it lies high and airy, with the distant river stealing steadily away to the ocean, like a man's life. To gain the milestone here, which the moss, primroses, violets, blue-bells, and wild roses, would soon render illegible bu for peering travellers pushing them aside with their sticks, you must come up a steep hill, come which way you may. So, all the tramps with carts or caravans—the Gipsy-tramp, the Show-tramp, the Cheap Jack—find it impossible to resist the temptations of the place, and all turn the horse loose when they come to it, and boil the pot. Bless the place, I love the ashes of the vagabond fires that have scorched its grass! What tramp children do I see here, attired in a handful of rags, making a gymnasium of the shafts of the cart, making a feather-bed of the flints and brambles, making a toy of the hobbled old horse who is not much more like a horse than any cheap toy would be! Here, do I encounter the cart of mats and brooms and baskets—with all thoughts of business given to the evening wind—with the stew made and being served out—with Cheap Jack and Dear Jill striking soft music out of the plates that are rattled like warlike cymbals when put up for auction at fairs and markets —their minds so influenced (no doubt) by the melody of the nightingales as they begin to sing in the woods behind them, that if I were to propose to deal, they would sell me anything at cost price. On this hallowed ground has it been my happy privilege (let me whisper it), to behold the White-haired Lady with the pink eyes, eating meat-pie with the Giant: while, by the hedge-side, on the box of blankets which I knew contained the snakes, were set forth the cups and saucers and the teapot. It was on an evening in August, that I chanced upon this ravishing spectacle, and I noticed that, whereas the Giant reclined half concealed beneath the overhanging boughs and seemed indifferent to Nature, the white hair of the gracious Lady streamed free in the breath of evening, and her pink eyes found pleasure in the landscape. I heard only a single sentence of her uttering, yet it bespoke a talent for modest repartee. The ill-mannered Giant—accursed be his evil race!—had interrupted the Lady in some remark, and, as I passed that enchanted corner of the wood, she gently reproved him, with the words, "Now, Cobby;"—Cobby! so short a name!—"ain't one fool enough to talk at a time?"

Within appropriate distance of this magic ground, though not so near it as that the song trolled from tap or bench at door, can invade its woodland silence, is a little hostelry which no man possessed of a penny was ever known to pass in warm weather. Before its entrance, are certain pleasant trimmed limes: likewise, a cool well, with so musical a bucket-handle that its fall upon the bucket rim will make a horse prick up his ears and neigh, upon the droughty road half a mile off. This is a house of great resort for haymaking tramps and harvest tramps, insomuch that they sit within, drinking their mugs of beer, their relinquished scythes and reaping-hooks glare out of the open windows, as if the whole establishment were a family war-coach of Ancient Britons. Later in the season, the whole country-side, for miles and miles, will swarm with hopping tramps. They come in families, men, women, and children, every family provided with a bundle of bedding, an iron pot, a number of babies, and too often with some poor sick creature quite unfit for the rough life, for whom they suppose the smell of the fresh hop to be a sovereign remedy. Many of these hoppers are Irish, but many come from London. They crowd all the roads, and camp under all the hedges and on all the scraps of common-land, and live among and upon the hops until they are all picked, and the hop-garden, so beautiful through the summer, look as if they had been laid waste by an invading army. Then, there is a vast exodus of tramps out of the county; and if you ride or drive round any turn of any road, at more than a foot pace, you will be bewildered to find that you have charged into the bosom of fifty families, and that there are splashing up all around you, in the utmost prodigality of confusion, bundles of bedding, babies, iron pots, and a good-humoured multitude of both sexes and all ages, equally divided between perspiration and intoxication.

XII.

DULLBOROUGH TOWN.

It lately happened that I found myself rambling about the scenes among which my earliest days were passed; scenes from which I departed when I was a child, and which I did not revisit until I was a man. This is no uncommon chance, but one that befals some of us any day; perhaps it may not be quite uninteresting to compare notes with the reader respecting an experience so familiar and a journey so uncommercial.

I call my boyhood's home (and I feel like a Tenor in an English Opera when I mention it) Dullborough. Most of us come from Dullborough who come from a country town.

As I left Dullborough in the days when there were no railroads in the land, I left it in a stage-coach. Through all the years that have since passed, have I ever lost the smell of the damp straw in which I was packed—like game—and forwarded, carriage paid, to the Cross Keys, Wood-street, Cheapside, London? There was no other inside passenger, and I consumed my sandwiches in solitude and dreariness, and it rained hard all the way and I thought life sloppier than I had expected to find it.

With this tender remembrance upon me, I was cavalierly shunted back into Dullborough the other day, by train. My ticket had been previously collected, like my taxes, and my shining new portmanteau had had a great plaster stuck upon it, and I had been defied by Act of Parliament to offer an objection to anything that was done to it, or me, under a penalty of not less than forty shillings or more than five pounds, compoundable for a term of imprisonment. When I had sent my disfigured property on to the hotel, I began to look about me; and the first discovery I made, was, that the Station had swallowed up the playing-field.

It was gone. The two beautiful hawthorn-trees, the hedge, the turf, and all those buttercups and daisies, had given place to the stoniest of jolting roads; while, beyond the Station, an ugly dark monster of a tunnel kept its jaws open, as if it had swallowed them and were ravenous for more destruction. The coach that had carried me away, was melodiously called Timpson's Blue-Eyed Maid, and belonged to Timpson, at the coach-office up-street; the locomotive engine that had brought me back, was called severely No. 97, and belonged to S. E. R., and was spitting ashes and hot-water over the blighted ground.

When I had been let out at the platform-door, like a prisoner whom his turnkey grudgingly released, I looked in again over the low wall, at the scene of departed glories. Here, in the haymaking time, had I been delivered from the dungeons of Seringapatam, an immense pile (of haycock), by my countrymen, the victorious British (boy next door and his two cousins), and had been recognised with ecstasy by my affianced one (Miss Green), who had come all the way from England (second house in the terrace) to ransom me, and marry me. Here, had I first heard in confidence, from one whose father was greatly connected, being under Government, of the existence of a terrible banditti, called "The Radicals," whose principles were, that the Prince Regent wore stays, and that nobody had a right to any salary, and that the army and navy ought to be put down—horrors at which I trembled in my bed, after supplicating that the Radicals might be speedily taken and hanged. Here, too, had we, the small boys of Boles's, had that cricket match against the small boys of Coles's, when Boles and Coles had actually met upon the ground, and when, instead of instantly hitting out at one another with the utmost fury, as we had all hoped and expected, those sneaks had said respectively, "I hope Mrs. Boles is well," and "I hope Mrs. Coles and the baby are doing charmingly." Could it be that, after all this, and much more, the Playing-field was a Station, and No. 97 expectorated boiling-water and redhot cinders on it, and the whole belonged by Act of Parliament to S. E. R. ?

As it could be, and was, I left the place with a heavy heart for a walk all over the town. And first of Timpson's up-street. When I departed from Dullborough in the strawy arms of Timpson's Blue-Eyed Maid, Timpson's was a moderate-sized coach-office (in fact, a little coach-office), with an oval transparency in the window, which looked beautiful by night, representing one of Timpson's coaches in the act of passing a milestone on the London road with great velocity, completely full inside and out, and all the passengers dressed in the first style of fashion, and enjoying themselves tremendously. I found no such place as Timpson's now—no such bricks and rafters, not to mention the name—no such edifice on the teeming earth. Pickford had come and knocked Timpson's down. Pickford had not only knocked Timpson's down, but had knocked two or three houses down on each side of Timpson's, and then had knocked the whole into one great establishment, with a pair of big gates, in and out of which, his (Pickford's) waggons are, in these days, always rattling, with their drivers sitting up so high, that they look in at the second floor windows of the old fashioned houses in the High-street as they shake the town. I have not the honour of Pickford's acquaintance, but I felt that he had done me an injury, not to say committed an act of boyslaughter, in running over my childhood in this rough manner; and if ever I meet Pickford driving one of his own monsters, and smoking a pipe the while (which is the custom of his men), he shall know by the expression of my eye, if it catches his, that there is something wrong between us.

Moreover, I felt that Pickford had no right to come rushing into Dullborough and deprive the town of a public picture. He is not Napoleon Bonaparte. When he took down the transparent stage-coach, he ought to have given the town a transparent van. With a gloomy conviction that Pickford is wholly utilitarian and unimaginative, I proceeded on my way.

It is a mercy I have not a red and green lamp and a night-bell at my door, for in my very young days I was taken to so many lyings-in that I wonder I escaped becoming a professional martyr to them in after-life. I suppose I had a very sympathetic nurse, with a large circle of married acquaintance. However that was, as I continued my walk through Dullborough, I found many houses to be solely associated in my mind with this particular interest. At one little greengrocer's shop, down certain steps from the street, I remembered to have waited on a lady who had had four children (I am afraid to write five, though I fully believe it was five) at a birth. This meritorious woman held quite a Reception in her room on the morning when I was introduced there, and the sight of the house brought vividly to my mind how the four (five) deceased young people lay, side by side, on a clean cloth on a chest of drawers: reminding me by a homely association, which I suspect their complexion to have assisted, of pigs' feet as they are usually displayed at a neat tripe-shop. Hot caudle was handed round on the occasion, and I further remembered as I stood contemplating the greengrocer's, that a subscription was entered into among the company, which became extremely alarming to my consciousness of having pocket-money on my person. This fact being known to my conductress, whoever she was, I was earnestly exhorted to contribute, but resolutely declined:

therein disgusting the company, who gave me to understand that I must dismiss all expectations of going to Heaven.

How does it happen that when all else is change wherever one goes, there yet seem, in every place, to be some few people who never alter? As the sight of the greengrocer's house recalled these trivial incidents of long ago, the identical greengrocer appeared on the steps, with his hands in his pockets, and leaning his shoulder against the door-post, as my childish eyes had seen him many a time; indeed, there was his old mark on the door-post yet, as if his shadow had become a fixture there. It was he himself; he might formerly have been an old-looking young man, or he might now be a young-looking old man, but there he was. In walking along the street, I had as yet looked in vain for a familiar face, or even a transmitted face; here was the very greengrocer who had been weighing and handling baskets on the morning of the reception. As he brought with him a dawning remembrance that he had had no proprietary interest in those babies, I crossed the road, and accosted him on the subject. He was not in the least excited or gratified, or in any way roused, by the accuracy of my recollection, but said, Yes, summut out of the common—he didn't remember how many it was (as if half a dozen babes either way made no difference) —had happened to a Mrs. What's-her-name, as once lodged there—but he didn't call it to mind, particular. Nettled by this phlegmatic conduct, I informed him that I had left the town when I was a child. He slowly returned, quite unsoftened, and not without a sarcastic kind of complacency, *Had* I? Ah! And did I find it had got on tolerably well without me? Such is the difference (I thought, when I had left him a few hundred yards behind, and was by so much in a better temper) between going away from a place and remaining in it. I had no right, I reflected, to be angry with the greengrocer for his want of interest. I was nothing to him: whereas he was the town, the cathedral, the bridge, the river, my childhood, and a large slice of my life, to me.

Of course the town had shrunk fearfully, since I was a child there. I had entertained the impression that the High-street was at least as wide as Regent-street, London, or the Italian Boulevard at Paris. I found it little better than a lane. There was a public clock in it, which I had supposed to be the finest clock in the world: whereas it now turned out to be as inexpressive, moon-faced, and weak a clock as ever I saw. It belonged to a Town Hall, where I had seen an Indian (who I now suppose wasn't an Indian) swallow a sword (which I now suppose he didn't). The edifice had appeared to me in those days so glorious a structure, that I had set it up in my mind as the model on which the Genie of the Lamp built the palace for Aladdin. A mean little brick heap, like a demented chapel, with a few yawning persons in leather gaiters, and in the last extremity for something to do, lounging at the door with their hands in their pockets, and calling themselve a Corn Exchange!

The Theatre was in existence, I found, on asking the fishmonger, who had a compact show of stock in his window, consisting of a sole and a quart of shrimps—and I resolved to comfort my mind by going to look at it. Richard the Third, in a very uncomfortable cloak, had first appeared to me there, and had made my heart leap with terror by backing up against the stage-box in which I was posted, while struggling for life against the virtuous Richmond. It was within those walls that I had learnt, as from a page of English history, how that wicked King slept in war-time on a sofa much too short for him, and how fearfully his conscience troubled his boots. There, too, had I first seen the funny countryman, but countryman of noble principles, in a flowered waistcoat, crunch up his little hat and throw it on the ground, and pull off his coat, saying, "Dom thee, squire, coom on with thy fistes then!" At which the lovely young woman who kept company with him (and who went out gleaning, in a narrow white muslin apron with five beautiful bars of five different coloured ribbons across it) was so frightened for his sake, that she fainted away. Many wondrous secrets of Nature had I come to the knowledge of in that sanctuary: of which not the least terrific were, that the witches in Macbeth bore an awful resemblance to the Thanes and other proper inhabitants of Scotland; and that the good King Duncan couldn't rest in his grave, but was constantly coming out of it, and calling himself somebody else. To the Theatre, therefore, I repaired for consolation. But I found very little, for it was in a bad and a declining way. A dealer in wine and bottled beer had already squeezed his trade into the box-office, and the theatrical money was taken—when it came—in a kind of meat-safe in the passage. The dealer in wine and bottled beer must have insinuated himself under the stage too; for he announced that he had various descriptions of alcoholic drinks "in the wood," and there was no possible stowage for the wood anywhere else. Evidently, he was by degrees eating the establishment away to the core, and would soon have sole possession of it. It was To Let, and hopelessly so, for its old purposes; and there had been no entertainment within its walls for a long time, except a Panorama; and even that had been announced as "pleasingly instructive," and I knew too well the fatal meaning and the leaden import of those terrible expressions. No, there was no comfort in the Theatre. It was mysteriously gone, like my own youth. Unlike my own youth, it might be coming back some day; but there was little promise of it.

As the town was placarded with references to the Dullborough Mechanics' Institution, I thought I would go and look at that establishment next. There had been no such thing in the town, in my young day, and it occurred to me that its extreme prosperity might have brought adversity upon the Drama. I found the Institution with some difficulty, and should scarcely have known that I had found it if I had judged from its external appearance only; but this was attributable to its never having been finished, and having no front: consequently, it led a modest and retired existence up a stable-yard. It was (as I learnt, on inquiry) a most flourishing Institution, and of the highest benefit to the town: two triumphs which I was glad to understand were not at all impaired by the seeming drawbacks that no mechanics belonged to it, and that it was steeped in debt to the chimney-pots. It had a large room, which was approached by an infirm step-ladder: the builder having declined to construct the intended staircase, without a present payment in cash, which Dullborough (though profoundly appreciative of the Institution) seemed unaccountably bashful about subscribing. The large room had cost—or would, when paid for—five hundred pounds; and it had more mortar in it and more echoes, than one might have expected to get for the money. It was fitted up with a platform, and the usual lecturing tools, including a large black board of a menacing appearance. On referring to lists of the courses of lectures that had been given in this thriving Hall, I fancied I detected a shyness in admitting that human nature when at leisure has any desire whatever to be relieved and diverted; and a furtive sliding in of any poor make-weight piece of amusement, shamefacedly and edgewise. Thus, I observed that it was necessary for the members to be knocked on the head with Gas, Air, Water, Food, the Solar System, the Geological periods, Criticism on Milton, the Steam-engine, John Bunyan, and Arrow-Headed Inscriptions, before they might be tickled by those unaccountable choristers, the negro singers in the court costume of the reign of George the Second. Likewise, that they must be stunned by a weighty inquiry whether there was internal evidence in Shakespeare's works, to prove that his uncle by the mother's side lived for some years at Stoke Newington, before they were brought-to by a Miscellaneous Concert.

But, indeed the masking of entertainment, and pretending it was something else—as people mask bedsteads when they are obliged to have them in sitting-rooms, and make believe that they are bookcases, sofas, chests of drawers, anything rather than bedsteads—was manifest even in the pretence of dreariness that the unfortunate entertainers themselves felt obliged in decency to put forth when they came here. One very agreeable professional singer who travelled with two professional ladies, knew better than to introduce either of those ladies to sing the ballad "Comin' through the Rye" without prefacing it himself, with some general remarks on wheat and clover; and even then, he dared not for his life call the song, a song, but disguised it in the bill as an "Illustration." In the library, also—fitted with shelves for three thousand books, and containing upwards of one hundred and seventy (presented copies mostly), seething their edges in damp plaster—there was such a painfully apologetic return of 62 offenders who had read Travels, Popular Biography, and mere Fiction descriptive of the aspirations of the hearts and souls of mere human creatures like themselves; and such an elaborate parade of 2 bright examples who had had down Euclid after the day's occupation and confinement; and 3 who had had down Metaphysics after ditto; and 1 who had had down Theology after ditto; and 4 who had worried Grammar, Political Economy, Botany, and Logarithms all at once after ditto; that I suspected the boasted class to be one man, who had been hired to do it.

Emerging from the Mechanics' Institution and continuing my walk about the town, I still noticed everywhere the prevalence, to an extraordinary degree, of this custom of putting the natural demand for amusement out of sight, as some untidy housekeepers put dust, and pretending that it was swept away. And yet it was ministered to, in a dull and abortive manner, by all who made this feint. Looking in at what is called in Dullborough "the serious bookseller's," where, in my childhood, I had studied the faces of numbers of gentlemen depicted in rostrums with a gaslight on each side of them, and casting my eyes over the open pages of certain printed discourses there, I found a vast deal of aiming at jocosity and dramatic effect, even in them—yes, verily, even on the part of one very wrathful expounder who bitterly anathematised a poor little Circus. Similarly, in the reading provided for the young people enrolled in the Lasso of Love, and other excellent unions, I found the writers generally under a distressing sense that they must start (at all events) like story-tellers, and delude the young persons into the belief that they were going to be interesting. As I looked in at this window for twenty minutes by the clock, I am in a position to offer a friendly remonstrance—not bearing on this particular point—to the designers and engravers of the pictures in those publications. Have they considered the awful consequences likely to flow from their representations of Virtue? Have they asked themselves the question, whether the terrific prospect of acquiring that fearful chubbiness of head, unwieldiness of arm, feeble dislocation of leg, crispiness of hair, and enormity of shirt-collar, which they represent as inseparable from Goodness, may not tend to confirm sensitive waverers, in Evil? A most impressive example (if I had believed it) of what a Dustman and a Sailor may come to, when they mend their ways, was presented to me in this same shop-window. When they were leaning (they were intimate friends) against a post, drunk and reckless, with surpassingly bad hats on, and their hair over their foreheads, they were rather picturesque, and looked as if they might be agreeable men if they would not be beasts. But, when they had got over their bad propensities, and when, as a consequence, their heads had swelled alarmingly, their hair had got so curly that it lifted their blown-out cheeks up, their coat-cuffs were so long that they never could do any work, and their eyes were so wide open that they never could do any sleep, they presented a spectacle calculated to plunge a timid nature into the depths of Infamy.

But, the clock that had so degenerated since I saw it last, admonished me that I had stayed here long enough; and I resumed my walk.

I had not gone fifty paces along the street when I was suddenly brought up by the sight of a man who got out of a little phaeton at the doctor's door, and went into the doctor's house. Immediately, the air was filled with the scent of trodden grass, and the perspective of years opened, and at the end of it was a little likeness of this man keeping a wicket, and I said, "God bless my soul! Joe Specks!"

Through many changes and much work, I had preserved a tenderness for the memory of Joe, forasmuch as we had made the acquaintance of Roderick Random together, and had believed him to be no ruffian, but an ingenuous and engaging hero. Scorning to ask the boy left in the phaeton whether it was really Joe, and scorning even to read the brass plate on the door—so sure was I—I rang the bell and informed the servant maid that a stranger sought audience of Mr. Specks. Into a room, half surgery, half study, I was shown to await his coming, and I found it, by a series of elaborate accidents, bestrewn with testimonies to Joe. Portrait of Mr. Specks, bust of Mr. Specks, silver cup from grateful patient to Mr. Specks, presentation sermon from local clergymen, dedication poem from local poet, dinner-card from local nobleman, tract on balance of power from local refugee, inscribed *Hommage de l'auteur à Specks.*

When my old schoolfellow came in, and I informed him with a smile that I was not a patient, he seemed rather at a loss to perceive any reason for smiling in connexion with that fact, and inquired to what was he to attribute the honour? I asked him, with another smile, could he remember me at all? He had not (he said) that pleasure. I was beginning to have but a poor opinion of Mr. Specks, when he said reflectively, "And yet there's a something too." Upon that, I saw a boyish light in his eyes that looked well, and I asked him if he could inform me, as a stranger who desired to know and had not the means of reference at hand, what the name of the young lady was, who married Mr. Random? Upon that, he said "Narcissa," and, after staring for a moment, called me by my name, shook me by the hand, and melted into a roar of laughter. "Why, of course, you'll remember Lucy Green," he said, after we had talked a little. "Of course," said I. "Whom do you think she married?" said he. "You?" I hazarded. "Me," said Specks, "and you shall see her." So I saw her, and she was fat, and if all the hay in the world had been heaped upon her, it could scarcely have altered her face more than Time had altered it from my remembrance of the face that had once looked down upon me into the fragrant dungeons of Seringapatam. But, when her youngest child came in after dinner (for I dined with them, and we had no other company than Specks, Junior, Barrister-at-Law, who went away as soon as the cloth was removed, to look after the young lady to whom he was going to be married next week), I saw again, in that little daughter, the little face of the hayfield, unchanged, and it quite touched my foolish heart. We talked immensely, Specks and Mrs. Specks, and I, and we spoke of our old selves as though our old selves were dead and gone, and indeed indeed they were —dead and gone, as the playing-field that had become a wilderness of rusty iron, and the property of S. E. R.

Specks, however, illuminated Dullborough with the rays of interest that I wanted and should otherwise have missed in it, and linked its present to its past, with a highly agreeable chain. And in Specks's society I had new occasion to observe what I had before noticed in similar communications among other men. All the schoolfellows and others of old, whom I inquired about, had either done superlatively well or superlatively ill— had either become uncertificated bankrupts, or been felonious and got themselves transported; or had made great hits in life, and done wonders. And this is so commonly the case, that I never can imagine what becomes of all the mediocre people of people's youth—especially, considering that we find no lack of the species in our maturity. But, I did not propound this difficulty to Specks, for no pause in the conversation gave me an occasion. Nor, could I discover one single flaw in the good doctor —when he reads this, he will receive in a friendly spirit the pleasantly meant record—except that he had forgotten his Roderick Random, and that he confounded Strap with Lieutenant Hatchway; who never knew Random, howsoever intimate with Pickles.

When I went alone to the Railway to catch my train at night (Specks had meant to go with me, but was inopportunely called out), I was in a more charitable mood with Dullborough than I had been all day; and yet in my heart I had loved it all day too. Ah! who was I that I should quarrel with the town for being changed to me, when I myself had came back, so changed, to it! All my early readings and early imaginations dated from this place, and I took them away so full of innocent construction and guileless belief, and I brought them back so worn and torn, so much the wiser and so much the worse!

XIII.

NIGHT WALKS.

Some years ago, a temporary inability to sleep, referable to a distressing impression, caused me to walk about the streets all night, for a series of several nights. The disorder might have taken a long time to conquer, if it had been faintly experimented on in bed; but, it was soon defeated by the brisk treatment of getting up directly after lying down, and going out, and coming home tired at sunrise.

In the course of those nights, I finished my education in a fair amateur experience of houselessness. My principal object being to get through the night, the pursuit of it brought me into sympathetic relations with people who have no other object every night in the year.

The month was March, and the weather damp, cloudy, and cold. The sun not rising before half-past five, the night perspective looked sufficiently long at half-past twelve: which was about my time for confronting it.

The restlessness of a great city, and the way in which it tumbles and tosses before it can get to sleep, formed one of the first entertainments offered to the contemplation of us houseless people. It lasted about two hours. We lost a great deal of companionship when the late public-houses turned their lamps out, and when the potmen thrust the last brawling drunkards into the street; but stray vehicles and stray people were left us, after that. If we were very lucky, a policeman's rattle sprang and a fray turned up; but, in general, surprisingly little of this diversion was provided. Except in the Haymarket, which is the worst kept part of London, and about Kent-street in the Borough, and along a portion of the line of the Old Kent-road, the peace was seldom violently broken. But, it was always the case that London, as if in imitation of individual citizens belonging to it, had expiring fits and starts of restlessness. After all seemed quiet, if one cab rattled by, half a dozen would surely follow; and Houselessness even observed that intoxicated people appeared to be magnetically attracted towards each other: so that we knew when we saw one drunken object staggering against the shutters of a shop, that another drunken object would stagger up before five minutes were out, to fraternise or fight with it. When we made a divergence from the regular species of drunkard, the thin-armed puff-faced leaden-lipped gin-drinker, and encountered a rarer specimen of a more decent appearance, fifty to one but that specimen was dressed in soiled mourning. As the street experience in the night, so the street experience in the day; the common folk who come unexpectedly into a little property, come unexpectedly into a deal of liquor.

At length these flickering sparks would die away, worn out—the last veritable sparks of waking life trailed from some late pieman or hot potato man—and London would sink to rest. And then the yearning of the houseless mind would be for any sign of company, any lighted place, any movement, anything suggestive of any one being up—nay, even so much as awake, for the houseless eye looked out for lights in windows.

Walking the streets under the pattering rain, Houselessness would walk and walk and walk, seeing nothing but the interminable tangle of streets, save at a corner, here and there, two policemen in conversation, or the sergeant or inspector looking after his men. Now and then in the night—but rarely—Houselessness would become aware of a furtive head peering out of a doorway a few yards before him, and, coming up with the head, would find a man standing bolt upright to keep within the doorway's shadow, and evidently intent upon no particular service to society. Under a kind of fascination, and in a ghostly silence suitable to the time, Houselessness and this gentleman would eye one another from head to foot, and so, without exchange of speech, part, mutually suspicious. Drip, drip, drip, from ledge and coping, splash from pipes and water-spouts, and by-and-by the houseless shadow would fall upon the stones that pave the way to Waterloo-bridge; it being in the houseless mind to have a halfpennyworth of excuse for saying "Good night" to the toll-keeper, and catching a glimpse of his fire. A good fire and a good great-coat and a good woollen neck-shawl, were comfortable things to see in conjunction with the toll-keeper; also his brisk wakefulness was excellent company when he rattled the change of halfpence down upon that metal table of his, like a man who defied the night, with all its sorrowful thoughts, and didn't care for the coming of dawn. There was need of encouragement on the threshold of the bridge, for the bridge was dreary. The chopped up murdered man, had not been lowered with a rope over the parapet when those nights were; he was alive, and slept then quietly enough most likely, and undisturbed by any dream of where he was to come. But the river had an awful look, the buildings on the banks were muffled in black shrouds, and the reflected lights seemed to originate deep in the water, as if the spectres of suicides were holding them to show where they went down. The wild moon and clouds were as restless as an evil conscience in a tumbled bed, and the very shadow of the immensity of London seemed to lie oppressively upon the river.

Between the bridge and the two great theatres, there was but the distance of a few hundred paces, so the theatres came next. Grim and black within, at night, those great dry Wells, and lonesome to imagine, with the rows of faces faded out, the lights extinguished, and the seats all empty. One would think that nothing in them knew itself at such a time but Yorick's skull. In one of my night walks, as the church steeples were shaking the March winds and rain with the strokes of Four, I passed the outer boundary of one of these great deserts, and entered it. With a dim lantern in my hand, I groped my well-known way to the stage and looked over the orchestra—which was like a great grave dug for a time of pestilence—into the void beyond. A dismal cavern of an immense aspect, with the chandelier gone dead like everything else, and nothing visible through mist and fog and space, but tiers of winding-sheets. The ground at my feet where, when last there, I had seen the peasantry of Naples dancing among the vines, reckless of the burning mountain which threatened to overwhelm them, was now in possession of a strong serpent of engine-hose, watchfully lying in wait for the serpent Fire, and ready to fly at it if it showed its forked tongue. A ghost of a watchman, carrying a faint corpse-candle, haunted the distant upper gallery and flitted away. Retiring within the proscenium, and holding my light above my head towards the rolled-up curtain—green no more, but black as ebony—my sight lost itself in a gloomy vault, showing faint indications in it of a shipwreck of canvas and cordage. Methought I felt much as a diver might, at the bottom of the sea.

In those small hours when there was no movement in the streets, it afforded matter for reflection to take Newgate in the way, and, touching its rough stone, to think of the prisoners in their sleep, and then to glance in at the lodge over the spiked wicket, and see the fire and light of the watching turnkeys, on the white wall. Not an inappropriate time either, to linger by that wicked little Debtors' Door—shutting tighter than any other door one ever saw—which has been Death's Door to so many. In the days of the uttering of forged one-pound notes by people tempted up from the country, how many hundreds of wretched creatures of both sexes—many quite innocent—swung out of a pitiless and inconsistent world, with the tower of yonder Christian church of Saint Sepulchre monstrously before their eyes! Is there any haunting of the Bank Parlour by the remorseful souls of old directors, in the nights of these later days, I wonder, or is it as quiet as this degenerate Aceldama of an Old Bailey?

To walk on to the Bank, lamenting the good old times and bemoaning the present evil period, would be an easy next step, so I would take it, and would make my houseless circuit of the Bank, and give a thought to the treasure within; likewise to the guard of soldiers passing the night there, and nodding over the fire. Next, I went to Billingsgate, in some hope of market-people, but it proving as yet too early, crossed London-bridge and got down by the water-side on the Surrey shore among the buildings of the great brewery. There was plenty going on at the brewery; and the reek, and the smell of grains, and the rattling of the plump dray horses at their mangers, were capital company. Quite refreshed by having mingled with this good society, I made a new start with a new heart, setting the old King's Bench prison before me for my next object, and resolving, when I should come to the wall, to think of poor Horace Kinch, and the Dry Rot in men.

A very curious disease the Dry Rot in men, and difficult to detect the beginning of. It had carried Horace Kinch inside the wall of the old King's Bench prison, and it had carried him out with his feet foremost. He was a likely man to look at, in the prime of life, well to do, as clever as he needed to be, and popular among many friends. He was suitably married, and had healthy and pretty children. But, like some fair-looking houses or fair-looking ships, he took the Dry Rot. The first strong external revelation of the Dry Rot in men, is a tendency to lurk and lounge; to be at street-corners without intelligible reason; to be going anywhere when met; to be about many places rather than at any; to do nothing tangible, but to have an intention of performing a variety of intangible duties to-morrow or the day after. When this manifestation of the disease is observed, the observer will usually connect it with a vague impression once formed or received, that the patient was living a little too hard. He will scarcely have had leisure to turn it over in his mind and form the terrible suspicion "Dry Rot," when he will notice a change for the worse in the patient's appearance: a certain slovenliness and deterioration, which is not poverty, nor dirt, nor intoxication, nor ill-health, but simply Dry Rot. To this, succeeds a smell as of strong waters, in the morning; to that, a looseness respecting money; to that, a stronger smell as of strong waters, at all times; to that, a looseness respecting everything; to that, a trembling of the limbs, somnolency, misery, and crumbling to pieces. As it is in wood, so it is in men. Dry Rot advances at a compound usury quite incalculable. A plank is found infected with it, and the whole structure is devoted. Thus t had been with the unhappy Horace Kinch, lately buried by a small subscription. Those who knew him had not nigh done saying, "So well off, so comfortably established, with such hope before him—and yet, it is feared, with a slight touch of Dry Rot!" when lo! the man was all Dry Rot and dust.

From the dead wall associated on those houseless nights with this too common story, I chose next to wander by Bethlehem Hospital; partly, because it lay on my road round to Westminster; partly, because I had a night fancy in my head which could be best pursued within sight of its walls and dome. And the fancy was this: Are not the sane and the insane equal at night as the sane lie a dreaming? Are not all of us outside this hospital, who dream, more or less in the condition of those inside it, every night of our lives? Are we not nightly persuaded, as they daily are, that we associate preposterously with kings and queens, emperors and empresses, and notabilities of all sorts? Do we not nightly jumble events and personages and times and places, as these do daily? Are we not sometimes troubled by our own sleeping inconsistencies, and do we not vexedly try to account for them or excuse them, just as these do sometimes in respect of their waking delusions? Said an afflicted man to me, when I was last in a hospital like this, "Sir, I can frequently fly." I was half ashamed to reflect that so could I—by night. Said a woman to me on the same occasion, "Queen Victoria frequently comes to dine with me, and her Majesty and I dine off peaches and maccaroni in our night-gowns, and his Royal Highness the Prince Consort does us the honour to make a third on horseback in a Field-Marshal's uniform." Could I refrain from reddening with consciousness when I remembered the amazing royal parties I myself had given (at night), the unaccountable viands I had put on table, and my extraordinary manner of conducting myself on those distinguished occasions? I wonder that the great master who knew everything, when he called Sleep the death of each day's life, did not call Dreams the insanity of each day's sanity.

By this time I had left the Hospital behind me, and was again setting towards the river; and in a short breathing space I was on Westminster-bridge, regaling my houseless eyes with the external walls of the British Parliament—the perfection of a stupendous institution, I know, and the admiration of all surrounding nations and succeeding ages, I do not doubt, but perhaps a little the better now and then for being pricked up to its work. Turning off into Old Palace-yard, the Courts of Law kept me company for a quarter of an hour; hinting in low whispers what numbers of people they were keeping awake, and how intensely wretched and horrible they were rendering the small hours to unfortunate suitors. Westminster Abbey was fine gloomy society for another quarter of an hour; suggesting a wonderful procession of its dead among the dark arches and pillars, each century more amazed by the century following it than by all the centuries going before. And indeed in those houseless night walks—which even included cemeteries where watchmen went round among the graves at stated times, and moved the tell-tale handle of an index which recorded that they had touched it at such an hour—it was a solemn consideration what enormous hosts of dead belong to one old great city, and how, if they were raised while the living slept, there would not be the space of a pin's point in all the streets and ways for the living to come out into. Not only that, but the vast armies of dead would overflow the hills and valleys beyond the city, and would stretch away all round it, God knows how far.

When a church clock strikes, on houseless ears in the dead of the night, it may be at first mistaken for company and hailed as such. But, as the spreading circles of vibration, which you may perceive at such a time with great clearness, go opening out, for ever and ever afterwards widening perhaps (as the philosopher has suggested) in eternal space, the mistake is rectified and the sense of loneliness is profounder. Once—it was after leaving the Abbey and turning my face north—I came to the great steps of Saint Martin's church as the clock was striking Three. Suddenly, a thing that in a moment more I should have trodden upon without seeing, rose up at my feet with a cry of loneliness and houselessness, struck out of it by the bell, the like of which I never heard. We then stood face to face looking at one another, frightened by one another. The creature was like a beetle-browed hair-lipped youth of twenty, and it had a loose bundle of rags on, which it held together with one of its hands. It shivered from head to foot, and its teeth chattered, and as it stared at me—persecutor, devil, ghost, whatever it thought me—it made with its whining mouth as if it were snapping at me, like a worried dog. Intending to give this ugly object, money, I put out my hand to stay it— for it recoiled as it whined and snapped—and laid my hand upon its shoulder. Instantly, it twisted out of its garment, like the young man in the New Testament, and left me standing alone with its rags in my hand.

Covent-garden Market, when it was market morning, was wonderful company. The great waggons of cabbages, with growers' men and boys lying asleep under them, and with sharp dogs from market-garden neighbourhoods looking after the whole, were as good as a party. But one of the worst night sights I know in London, is to be found in the children who prowl about this place; who sleep in the baskets, fight for the offal, dart at any object they think they can lay their thieving hands on, dive under the carts and barrows, dodge the constables, and are perpetually making a blunt pattering on the pavement of the Piazza with the rain of their naked feet. A painful and unnatural result comes of the comparison one is forced to institute between the growth of corruption as displayed in the so much improved and cared for fruits of the earth, and the growth of corruption as displayed in these all uncared for (except inasmuch as ever-hunted) savages.

There was early coffee to be got about Covent-garden Market, and that was more company—warm company, too, which was better. Toast of a very substantial quality, was likewise procurable: though the towzled-headed man who made it, in an inner chamber within the coffee-room, hadn't got his coat on yet, and was so heavy with sleep that in every interval of toast and coffee he went off anew behind the partition into complicated cross-roads of choke and snore, and lost his way directly. Into one of these establishments (among the earliest) near Bow-street, there came, one morning as I sat over my houseless cup, pondering where to go next, a man in a high and long snuff-coloured coat, and shoes, and, to the best of my belief, nothing else but a hat, who took out of his hat a large cold meat pudding; a meat pudding so large that it was a very tight fit, and brought the lining of the hat out with it. This mysterious man was known by his pudding, for, on his entering, the man of sleep brought him a pint of hot tea, a small loaf, and a large knife and fork and plate. Left to himself in his box, he stood the pudding on the bare table, and, instead of cutting it, stabbed it, over-hand, with the knife, like a mortal enemy; then took the knife out, wiped it on his sleeve, tore the pudding asunder with his fingers, and ate it all up. The remembrance of this man with the pudding remains with me as the remembrance of the most spectral person my houselessness encountered. Twice only was I in that establishment, and twice I saw him stalk in (as I should say, just out of bed, and presently going back to bed), take out his pudding, stab his pudding, wipe the dagger, and eat his pudding all up. He was a man whose figure promised cadaverousness, but who had an excessively red face, though shaped like a horse's. On the second occasion of my seeing him, he said, huskily to the man of sleep, "Am I red to-night?" "You are," he uncompromisingly answered. "My mother," said the spectre, "was a red-faced woman that liked drink, and I looked at her hard when she laid in her coffin, and I took the complexion." Somehow, the pudding seemed an unwholesome pudding after that, and I put myself in its way no more.

When there was no market, or when I wanted variety, a railway terminus with the morning mails coming in, was remunerative company. But like most of the company to be had in this world, it lasted only a very short time. The station lamps would burst out ablaze, the porters would emerge from places of concealment, the cabs and trucks would rattle to their places (the post-office carts were already in theirs), and, finally, the bell would strike up, and the train would come banging in. But, there were few passengers and little luggage, and everything scuttled away with the greatest expedition. The locomotive post-offices, with their great nets—as if they had been dragging the country for bodies—would fly open as to their doors, and would disgorge a smell of lamp, an exhausted clerk, a guard in a red coat, and their bags of letters; the engine would blow and heave and perspire, like an engine wiping its forehead and saying what a run it had had; and within ten minutes the lamps were out, and I was houseless and alone again.

But now, there were driven cattle on the high road near, wanting (as cattle always do) to turn into the midst of stone walls, and squeeze themselves through six inches' width of iron railing, and getting their heads down (also as cattle always do) for tossing-purchase at quite imaginary dogs, and giving themselves and every devoted creature associated with them a most extraordinary amount of unnecessary trouble. Now, too, the conscious gas began to grow pale with the knowledge that daylight was coming, and straggling workpeople were already in the streets, and, as waking life had become extinguished with the last pieman's sparks, so it began to be rekindled with the fires of the first street corner breakfast-sellers. And so by faster and faster degrees, until the last degrees were very fast, the day came, and I was tired and could sleep. And it is not, as I used to think, going home at such times, the least wonderful thing in London, that in the real desert region of the night, the houseless wanderer is alone there. I knew well enough where to find Vice and Misfortune of all kinds, if I had chosen; but they were put out of sight, and my houselessness had many miles upon miles of streets in which it could, and did, have its own solitary way.

XIV.

CHAMBERS.

HAVING occasion to transact some business with a solicitor who occupies a highly suicidal set of chambers in Gray's Inn, I afterwards took a turn in the large square of that stronghold of Melancholy, reviewing, with congenial surroundings, my experiences of Chambers.

I began, as was natural, with the Chambers I had just left. They were an upper set on a rotten staircase, with a mysterious bunk or bulkhead on the landing outside them, of a rather nautical and Screw Collier-like appearance than otherwise, and painted an intense black. Many dusty years have passed, since the appropriation of this Davy Jones's locker to any purpose, and during the whole period within the memory of living man, it has been hasped and padlocked. I cannot quite satisfy my mind whether it was originally meant for the reception of coals, or bodies, or as a place of temporary security for the plunder "looted" by laundresses; but I incline to the last opinion. It is about breast-high, and usually serves as a bulk for defendants in reduced circumstances to lean against and ponder at, when they come on the hopeful errand of trying to make an arrangement without money—under which auspicious circumstances it mostly happens that the legal gentleman they want to see, is much engaged, and they pervade the staircase for a considerable period. Against this opposing bulk, in the absurdest manner, the tomb-like outer door of the solicitor's chambers (which is also of an intense black) stands in dark ambush, half open, and half shut, all day. The solicitor's apartments are three in number; consisting of a slice, a cell, and a wedge. The slice is assigned to the two clerks, the cell is occupied by the principal, and the wedge is devoted to stray papers, old game baskets from the country, a washing-stand, and a model of a patent Ship's Caboose which was exhibited in Chancery at the commencement of the present century on an application for an injunction to restrain infringement. At about half-past nine on every week-day morning, the younger of the two clerks (who, I have reason to believe, leads the fashion at Pentonville in the articles of pipes and shirts) may be found knocking the dust out of his official door-key on the bunk or locker before mentioned; and so exceedingly subject to dust is his key, and so very retentive of that superfluity, that in exceptional summer weather when a ray of sunlight has fallen on the locker in my presence, I have noticed its inexpressive countenance to be deeply marked by a kind of Bramah erysipelas or small-pox.

This set of chambers (as I have gradually discovered, when I have had restless occasion to make inquiries or leave messages, after office hours) is under the charge of a lady named Sweeney, in figure extremely like an old family-umbrella: whose dwelling confronts a dead wall in a court off Gray's Inn-lane, and who is usually fetched into the passage of that bower, when wanted, from some neighbouring home of industry, which has the curious property of imparting an inflammatory appearance to her visage. Mrs. Sweeney is one of the race of professed laundresses, and is the compiler of a remarkable manuscript volume entitled "Mrs. Sweeney's Book," from which much curious statistical information may be gathered respecting the high prices and small uses of soda, soap, sand, firewood, and other such articles. I have created a legend in my mind—and consequently I believe it with the utmost pertinacity—that the late Mr. Sweeney was a ticket-porter under the Honourable Society of Gray's Inn, and that, in consideration of his long and valuable services, Mrs. Sweeney was appointed to her present post. For, though devoid of personal charms, I have observed this lady to exercise a fascination over the elderly ticket-porter mind (particularly under the gateway, and in corners and entries), which I can only refer to her being one of the fraternity, yet not competing with it. All that need be said concerning this set of chambers, is said, when I have added that it is in a large double house in Gray's Inn-square, very much out of repair, and that the outer portal is ornamented in a hideous manner with certain stone remains, which have the appearance of the dismembered bust, torso, and limbs, of a petrified bencher.

Indeed, I look upon Gray's Inn generally as one of the most depressing institutions in brick and mortar, known to the children of men. Can anything be more dreary than its arid Square, Saharah Desert of the law, with the ugly old tiled-topped tenements, the dirty windows, the bills To Let To Let, the door-posts inscribed like gravestones, the crazy gateway giving upon the filthy Lane, the scowling iron-barred prison-like passage into Verulam-buildings, the mouldy red-nosed ticket-porters with little coffin plates and why with aprons, the dry hard atomy-like appearance of the whole dust-heap? When my un-commercial travels tend to this dismal spot, my comfort is, its rickety state. Imagination gloats over the fulness of time, when the staircases shall have quite tumbled down—they are daily wearing into an ill-savoured powder, but have not quite tumbled down yet—when the last old prolix bencher all of the olden time, shall have been got out of an upper window by means of a Fire-Ladder, and carried off to the Holborn Union; when the last clerk shall have engrossed the last parchment behind the last splash on the last of the mud-stained windows, which, all through the miry year, are pilloried out of recognition in Gray's Inn-lane. Then, shall a squalid little trench, with rank grass and a pump in it, lying between the coffee-house and South-square, be wholly given up to cats and rats, and not, as now, have its empire divided between those animals and a few briefless bipeds—surely called to the Bar by voices of deceiving spirits, seeing that they are wanted there by no mortal—who glance down, with eyes better glazed than their casements, from their dreary and lacklustre rooms. Then shall the way Nor' Westward, now lying under a short grim colonnade where in summer time pounce flies from law-stationering windows into the eyes of laymen, be choked with rubbish and happily become impassable. Then shall the gardens where turf, trees, and gravel wear a legal livery of black, run rank, and pilgrims go to Gorhambury to see Bacon's effigy as he sat, and not come here (which in truth they seldom do) to see where he walked. Then, in a word, shall the old-established vendor of periodicals sit alone in his little crib of a shop behind the Holborn Gate, like that lumbering Marius among the ruins of Carthage, who has sat heavy on a thousand million of similes.

At one period of my uncommercial career I much frequented another set of chambers in Gray's Inn-square. They were what is familiarly called "a top set," and all the eatables and drinkables introduced into them acquired a flavour of Cockloft. I have known an unopened Strasbourg pâté fresh from Fortnum and Mason's, to draw in this cockloft tone through its crockery dish, and become penetrated with cockloft to the core of its inmost truffle in three-quarters of an hour. This, however, was not the most curious feature of those chambers; that, consisted in the profound conviction entertained by my esteemed friend Parkle (their tenant) that they were clean. Whether it was an inborn hallucination, or whether it was imparted to him by Mrs. Miggot the laundress, I never could ascertain. But, I believe he would have gone to the stake upon the question. Now, they were so dirty that I could take off the distinctest impression of my figure on any article of furniture by merely lounging upon it for a few moments; and it used to be a private amusement of mine to print myself off—if I may use the expression—all over the rooms. It was the first large circulation I had. At other times I have accidentally shaken a window-curtain while in animated conversation with Parkle, and struggling insects which were certainly red, and were certainly not ladybirds, have dropped on the back of my hand. Yet Parkle lived in that top set years, bound body and soul to the superstition that they were clean. He used to say, when congratulated upon them, "Well, they are not like chambers in one respect, you know; they are clean." Concurrently, he had an idea which he could never explain, that Mrs. Miggot was in some way connected with the Church. When he was in particularly good spirits, he used to believe that a deceased uncle of hers had been a Dean; when he was poorly and low, he believed that her brother had been a Curate. I and Mrs. Miggot (she was a genteel woman) were on confidential terms, but I never knew her to commit herself to any distinct assertion on the subject; she merely claimed a proprietorship in the Church, by looking when it was mentioned, as if the reference awakened the slumbering Past, and were personal. It may have been his amiable confidence in Mrs. Miggot's better days that inspired my friend with his delusion respecting the chambers, but he never wavered in his fidelity to it for a moment, though he wallowed in dirt seven years.

Two of the windows of these chambers looked down

into the garden; and we have sat up there together, many a summer evening, saying how pleasant it was, and talking of many things. To my intimacy with that top set, I am indebted for three of my liveliest personal impressions of the loneliness of life in chambers. They shall follow here, in order; first, second, and third.

First. My Gray's Inn friend, on a time, hurt one of his legs, and it became seriously inflamed. Not knowing of his indisposition, I was on my way to visit him as usual, one summer evening, when I was much surprised by meeting a lively leech in Field-court, Gray's Inn, seemingly on his way to the West End of London. As the leech was alone, and was of course unable to explain his position, even if he had been inclined to do so (which he had not the appearance of being), I passed him and went on. Turning the corner of Gray's Inn-square, I was beyond expression amazed by meeting another leech —also entirely alone, and also proceeding in a westerly direction, though with less decision of purpose. Ruminating on this extraordinary circumstance, and endeavouring to remember whether I had ever read, in the Philosophical Transactions or any work on Natural History, of a migration of Leeches, I ascended to the top set, past the dreary series of closed outer doors of offices and an empty set or two, which intervened between that lofty region and the surface. Entering my friend's rooms, I found him stretched upon his back, like Prometheus Bound, with a perfectly demented ticket-porter in attendance on him instead of the Vulture: which helpless individual, who was feeble and frightened, had (my friend explained to me, in great choler) been endeavouring for some hours to apply leeches to his leg, and as yet had only got on two out of twenty. To this Unfortunate's distraction between a damp cloth on which he had placed the leeches to freshen them, and the wrathful adjurations of my friend to "Stick 'em on, sir!" I referred the phenomenon I had encountered: the rather as two fine specimens were at that moment going out at the door, while a general insurrection of the rest was in progress on the table. After a while our united efforts prevailed, and, when the leeches came off and had recovered their spirits, we carefully tied them up in a decanter. But I never heard more of them than that they were all gone next morning, and that the Out-of-door young man of Bickle Bush and Bodger, on the ground floor, had been bitten and blooded by some creature not identified. They never "took" on Mrs. Miggot, the laundress; but, I have always preserved fresh, the belief that she unconsciously carried several about her, until they gradually found openings in life.

Second. On the same staircase with my friend Parkle, and on the same floor, there lived a man of law who pursued his business elsewhere, and used those chambers as his place of residence. For three or four years, Parkle rather knew of him than knew him, but after that—for Englishmen—short pause of consideration, they began to speak. Parkle exchanged words with him in his private character only, and knew nothing of his business ways, or means. He was a man a good deal about town, but always alone. We used to remark to one another, that although we often encountered him in theatres, concert-rooms, and similar public places, he was always alone. Yet he was not a gloomy man, and was of a decidedly conversational turn; insomuch that he would sometimes of an evening lounge with a cigar in his mouth, half in and half out of Parkle's rooms, and discuss the topics of the day by the hour. He used to hint on these occasions that he had four faults to find with life; firstly, that it obliged a man to be always winding up his watch; secondly, that London was too small; thirdly, that it therefore wanted variety; fourthly, that there was too much dust in it. There was so much dust in his own faded chambers, certainly, that they reminded me of a sepulchre, furnished in prophetic anticipation of the present time, which had newly been brought to light, after having lain buried a few thousand years. One dry hot autumn evening at twilight, this man, being then five years turned of fifty, looked in upon Parkle in his usual lounging way, with his cigar in his mouth as usual, and said, "I am going out of town." As he never went out of town, Parkle said, "Oh indeed! At last?" "Yes," says he, "at last. For what is a man to do? London is so small! If you go West, you come to Hounslow. If you go East, you come to Bow. If you go South, there's Brixton or Norwood. If you go North, you can't get rid of Barnet. Then, the monotony of all the streets, streets, streets—and of all the roads, roads, roads—and the dust, dust, dust!" When he had said this, he wished Parkle a good evening, but came back again and said, with his watch in his hand, "Oh, I really cannot go on winding up this watch over and over again; I wish you would take care of it." So, Parkle laughed and consented, and the man went out of town. The man remained out of town so long, that his letter-box became choked, and no more letters could be got into it, and they began to be left at the lodge and to accumulate there. At last the head-porter decided, on conference with the steward, to use his master-key and look into the chambers, and give them the benefit of a whiff of air. Then, it was found that he had hanged himself to his bedstead, and had left this written memorandum: "I should prefer to be cut down by my neighbour and friend (if he will allow me to call him so), H. Parkle, Esq." This was the end of Parkle's occupancy of chambers. He went into lodgings immediately.

Third. While Parkle lived in Gray's Inn, and I myself was uncommercially preparing for the Bar—which is done, as everybody knows, by having a frayed old gown put on in a pantry by an old woman in a chronic state of Saint Anthony's fire and dropsy, and, so decorated, bolting a bad dinner in a party of four, whereof each individual mistrusts the other three—I say, while these things were, there was a certain elderly gentleman who lived in a court of the Temple, and was a great judge and lover of port wine. Every day, he dined at his club and drank his bottle or two of port wine, and every night came home to the Temple and went to bed in his lonely chambers. This had gone on many years without variation, when one night he had a fit on coming home, and fell and cut his head deep, but partly recovered and groped about in the dark to find the door. When he was afterwards discovered, dead, it was clearly established by the marks of his hands about the room that he must have done so. Now, this chanced on the night of Christmas Eve, and over him lived a young fellow who had sisters and young country-friends, and who gave them a little party that night, in the course of which they played at Blindman's Buff. They played that game, for their greater sport, by the light of the fire only; and once when they were all quietly rustling and stealing about, and the blindman was trying to pick out the prettiest sister (for which I am far from blaming him), somebody cried, Hark! The man below must be playing Blindman's Buff by himself to-night! They listened, and they heard sounds of some one falling about and stumbling against furniture, and they all laughed at the conceit, and went on with their play, more light-hearted and merry than ever. Thus, those two so different games of life and death were played out together, blindfold, in the two sets of chambers.

Such are the occurrences which, coming to my knowledge, imbued me long ago with a strong sense of the loneliness of chambers. There was a fantastic illustration to much the same purpose implicitly believed by a strange sort of man now dead, whom I knew when I had not quite arrived at legal years of discretion, though I was already in the uncommercial line.

This was a man who, though not more than thirty, had seen the world in divers irreconcilable capacities— had been an officer in a South American regiment among other odd things—but had not achieved much in any way of life, and was in debt, and in hiding. He occupied chambers of the dreariest nature in Lyons Inn; his name, however, was not upon the door, or door-post, but in lieu of it stood the name of a friend who had died in the chambers, and had given him the furniture. The story arose out of the furniture, and was to this effect:—Let the former holder of the chambers whose name was still upon the door and door-post, be Mr. Testator.

Mr. Testator took a set of chambers in Lyons Inn when he had but very scanty furniture for his bedroom, and none for his sitting-room. He had lived some wintry months in this condition, and had found it very bare and cold. One night, past midnight, when he sat writing and still had writing to do that must be done before he went to bed, he found himself out of coals. He had coals down stairs, but had never been to his cellar; however, the cellar-key was on his mantelshelf, and if he went down and opened the cellar it fitted, he might fairly assume the coals in that cellar to be his. As to his laundress, she lived among the coal-waggons and Thames watermen—for there were Thames watermen at that time—in some unknown rat-hole by the river, down lanes and alleys on the other side of the Strand. As to any other person to meet him or obstruct him, Lyons Inn was dreaming, drunk, maudlin, moody, betting, brooding over bill-discounting or renewing—asleep or awake, minding its own affairs. Mr. Testator took his coal-scuttle in one hand, his candle and key in the other, and descended to the dismallest underground dens of

Lyons Inn, where the late vehicles in the streets became thunderous, and all the water-pipes in the neighbourhood seemed to have Macbeth's Amen sticking in their throats, and to be trying to get it out. After groping here and there among low doors to no purpose, Mr. Testator at length came to a door with a rusty padlock which his key fitted. Getting the door open with much trouble, and looking in, he found, no coals, but a confused pile of furniture. Alarmed by this intrusion on another man's property, he locked the door again, found his own cellar, filled his scuttle, and returned up-stairs.

But the furniture he had seen, ran on castors across and across Mr. Testator's mind incessantly, when, in the chill hour of five in the morning he got to bed. He particularly wanted a table to write at, and a table expressly made to be written at, had been the piece of furniture in the foreground of the heap. When his laundress emerged from her burrow in the morning to make his kettle boil, he artfully led up to the subject of cellars and furniture; but the two ideas had evidently no connexion in her mind. When she left him, and he sat at his breakfast, thinking about the furniture, he recalled the rusty state of the padlock, and inferred that the furniture must have been stored in the cellars for a long time — was perhaps forgotten — owner dead, perhaps? After thinking it over, a few days, in the course of which he could pump nothing out of Lyons Inn about the furniture, he became desperate, and resolved to borrow that table. He did so, that night. He had not had the table long, when he determined to borrow an easy-chair; he had not had that long, when he made up his mind to borrow a bookcase; then, a couch; then, a carpet and rug. By that time, he felt he was "in furniture stepped in so far," as that it could be no worse to borrow it all. Consequently, he borrowed it all, and locked up the cellar for good. He had always locked it, after every visit. He had carried up every separate article in the dead of the night, and, at the best, had felt as wicked as a Resurrection Man. Every article was blue and furry when brought into his rooms, and he had had, in a murderous and guilty sort of way, to polish it up while London slept.

Mr. Testator lived in his furnished chambers two or three years, or more, and gradually lulled himself into the opinion that the furniture was his own. This was his convenient state of mind when, late one night, a step came up the stairs, and a hand passed over his door feeling for his knocker, and then one deep and solemn rap was rapped that might have been a spring in Mr. Testator's easy-chair to shoot him out of it: so promptly was it attended with that effect.

With a candle in his hand, Mr. Testator went to the door, and found there, a very pale and very tall man; a man who stooped; a man with very high shoulders, a very narrow chest, and a very red nose; a shabby genteel man. He was wrapped in a long threadbare black coat, fastened up the front with more pins than buttons, and under his arm he squeezed an umbrella without a handle, as if he were playing bagpipes. He said, "I ask your pardon, but can you tell me——" and stopped; his eyes resting on some object within the chambers.

"Can I tell you what?" asked Mr. Testator, noting this stoppage with quick alarm.

"I ask your pardon," said the stranger, "but—this is not the inquiry I was going to make—*do* I see in there, any small article of property belonging to *me?*"

Mr. Testator was beginning to stammer that he was not aware—when the visitor slipped past him, into the chambers. There, in a goblin way which froze Mr. Testator to the marrow, he examined, first, the writing-table, and said, "Mine;" then, the easy-chair, and said, "Mine;" then, the bookcase, and said, "Mine;" then, turned up a corner of the carpet, and said, "Mine!" in a word, inspected every item of furniture from the cellar, in succession, and said, "Mine!" Towards the end of this investigation, Mr. Testator perceived that he was sodden with liquor, and that the liquor was gin. He was not unsteady with gin, either in his speech or carriage; but he was stiff with gin in both particulars.

Mr. Testator was in a dreadful state, for (according to his making out of the story) the possible consequences of what he had done in recklessness and hardihood, flashed upon him in their fulness for the first time. When they had stood gazing at one another for a little while, he tremulously began:

"Sir, I am conscious that the fullest explanation, compensation, and restitution, are your due. They shall be yours. Allow me to entreat that, without temper, without even natural irritation on your part, we may have a little——"

"Drop of something to drink," interposed the stranger. "I am agreeable."

Mr. Testator had intended to say, "a little quiet conversation," but with great relief of mind adopted the amendment. He produced a decanter of gin, and was bustling about for hot water and sugar, when he found that his visitor had already drunk half of the decanter's contents. With hot water and sugar the visitor drank the remainder before he had been an hour in the chambers by the chimes of the church of St. Mary in the Strand; and during the process he frequently whispered to himself, "Mine!"

The gin gone, and Mr. Testator wondering what was to follow it, the visitor rose and said, with increased stiffness, "At what hour of the morning, sir, will it be convenient?" Mr. Testator hazarded, "At ten?" "Sir," said the visitor, "at ten, to the moment, I shall be here." He then contemplated Mr. Testator somewhat at leisure, and said, "God bless you! How is your wife?" Mr. Testator (who never had a wife) replied with much feeling, "Deeply anxious, poor soul, but otherwise well." The visitor thereupon turned and went away, and fell twice in going down stairs. From that hour he was never heard of. Whether he was a ghost, or a spectral illusion of conscience, or a drunken man who had no business there, or the drunken rightful owner of the furniture, with a transitory gleam of memory; whether he got safe home, or had no home to get to; whether he died of liquor on the way, or lived in liquor ever afterwards; he never was heard of more. This was the story, received with the furniture and held to be as substantial, by its second possessor in an upper set of chambers in grim Lyons Inn.

It is to be remarked of chambers in general, that they must have been built for chambers, to have the right kind of loneliness. You may make a great dwelling-house very lonely, by isolating suites of rooms and calling them chambers, but you cannot make the true kind of loneliness. In dwelling-houses, there have been family festivals; children have grown in them, girls have bloomed into women in them, courtships and marriages have taken place in them. True chambers never were young, childish, maidenly; never had dolls in them, or rocking-horses, or christenings, or betrothals, or little coffins. Let Gray's Inn identify the child who first touched hands and hearts with Robinson Crusoe, in any one of its many "sets," and that child's little statue, in white marble with a golden inscription, shall be at its service, at my cost and charge, as a drinking fountain for the spirit, to freshen its thirsty square. Let Lincoln's produce from all its houses, a twentieth of the procession derivable from any dwelling-house one twentieth of its age, of fair young brides who married for love and hope, not settlements, and all the Vice-Chancellors shall thenceforward be kept in nosegays for nothing, on application to the writer hereof. It is not denied that on the terrace of the Adelphi, or in any of the streets of that subterranean-stable-haunted spot, or about Bedford-row, or James-street of that ilk (a grewsome place), or anywhere among the neighbourhoods that have done flowering and have run to seed, you may find Chambers replete with the accommodations of Solitude, Closeness, and Darkness, where you may be as low-spirited as in the genuine article, and might be as easily murdered, with the placid reputation of having merely gone down to the sea-side. But, the many waters of life did run musical in those dry channels once;—among the Inns, never. The only popular legend known in relation to any one of the dull family of Inns, is a dark Old Bailey whisper concerning Clement's, and importing how the black creature who holds the sun-dial there, was a negro who slew his master and built the dismal pile out of the contents of his strong-box—for which architectural offence alone he ought to have been condemned to live in it. But, what populace would waste fancy upon such a place, or on New Inn, Staple Inn, Barnard's Inn, or any of the shabby crew?

The genuine laundress, too, is an institution not to be had in its entirety out of and away from the genuine Chambers. Again, it is not denied that you may be robbed elsewhere. Elsewhere you may have—for money—dishonesty, drunkenness, dirt, laziness, and profound in capacity. But the veritable shining-red-faced, shameless laundress; the true Mrs. Sweeney—in figure, colour, texture, and smell, like the old damp family umbrella; the tip-top complicated abomination of stockings, spirits, bonnet, limpness, looseness, and larceny; is only to be drawn at the fountain-head. Mrs. Sweeney is beyond the reach of individual art. It requires the united efforts of several men to ensure that great result, and it is only developed in perfection under an Honourable Society and in an Inn of Court.

XV.

NURSE'S STORIES.

THERE are not many places that I find it more agreeable to revisit when I am in an idle mood, than some places to which I have never been. For, my acquaintance with those spots is of such long standing, and has ripened into an intimacy of so affectionate a nature, that I take a particular interest in assuring myself that they are unchanged.

I never was in Robinson Crusoe's Island, yet I frequently return there. The colony he established on it soon faded away, and it is uninhabited by any descendants of the grave and courteous Spaniards, or of Will Atkins and the other mutineers, and has relapsed into its original condition. Not a twig of its wicker houses remains, its goats have long run wild again, its screaming parrots would darken the sun with a cloud of many flaming colours if a gun were fired there, no face is ever reflected in the waters of the little creek which Friday swam across when pursued by his two brother cannibals with sharpened stomachs. After comparing notes with other travellers who have similarly revisited the Island

and conscientiously inspected it, I have satisfied myself that it contains no vestige of Mr. Atkins's domesticity or theology, though his track on the memorable evening of his landing to set his captain ashore, when he was decoyed about and round about until it was dark, and his boat was stove, and his strength and spirits failed him, is yet plainly to be traced. So is the hill-top on which Robinson was struck dumb with joy when the reinstated captain pointed to the ship, riding within half a mile of the shore, that was to bear him away, in the nine-and-twentieth year of his seclusion in that lonely place. So is the sandy beach on which the memorable footstep was impressed, and where the savages hauled up their canoes when they came ashore for those dreadful public dinners, which led to a dancing worse than speech-making. So is the cave where the flaring eyes of the old goat made such a goblin appearance in the dark. So is the site of the hut where Robinson lived with the dog and the parrot and the cat, and where he endured those first agonies of solitude, which—strange to say—never involved any ghostly fancies; a circumstance so very remarkable, that perhaps he left out something in writing his record? Round hundreds of such objects, hidden in the dense tropical foliage, the tropical sea breaks evermore; and over them the tropical sky, saving in the short rainy season, shines bright and cloudless.

Neither, was I ever belated among wolves, on the borders of France and Spain; nor, did I ever, when night was closing in and the ground was covered with snow, draw up my little company among some felled trees which served as a breastwork, and there fire a train of gunpowder so dexterously that suddenly we had three or four score blazing wolves illuminating the darkness around us. Nevertheless, I occasionally go back to that dismal region and perform the feat again; when indeed to smell the singeing and the frying of the wolves afire, and to see them setting one another alight as they rush and tumble, and to behold them rolling in the snow vainly attempting to put themselves out, and to hear their howlings taken up by all the echoes as well as by all the unseen wolves within the woods, makes me tremble.

I was never in the robbers' cave, where Gil Blas lived, but I often go back there and find the trap-door just as heavy to raise as it used to be, while that wicked old disabled Black lies everlastingly cursing in bed. I was never in Don Quixote's study where he read his books of chivalry until he rose and hacked at imaginary giants, and then refreshed himself with great draughts of water, yet you couldn't move a book in it without my knowledge, or with my consent. I was never (thank Heaven) in company with the little old woman who hobbled out of the chest and told the merchant Abudah to go in search of the Talisman of Oromanes, yet I make it my business to know that she is well preserved and as intolerable as ever. I was never at the school where the boy Horatio Nelson got out of bed to steal the pears: not because he wanted any, but because every other boy was afraid: yet I have several times been back to this Academy, to see him let down out of window with a sheet. So with Damascus, and Bagdad, and Brobdingnag (which has the curious fate of being usually misspelt when written), and Lilliput, and Laputa, and the Nile, and Abyssinia, and the Ganges, and the North Pole, and many hundreds of places—I was never at them, yet it is an affair of my life to keep them intact, and I am always going back to them.

But, when I was in Dullborough one day, revisiting the associations of my childhood as recorded in previous pages of these notes, my experience in this wise was made quite inconsiderable and of no account, by the quantity of places and people—utterly impossible places and people, but none the less alarmingly real—that I found I had been introduced to by my nurse before I was six years old, and used to be forced to go back to at night without at all wanting to go. If we all knew our own minds (in a more enlarged sense than the popular acceptation of that phrase), I suspect we should find our nurses responsible for most of the dark corners we are forced to go back to, against our wills.

The first diabolical character who intruded himself on my peaceful youth (as I called to mind that day at Dullborough), was a certain Captain Murderer. This wretch must have been an offshoot of the Blue Beard family, but I had no suspicion of the consanguinity in those times. His warning name would seem to have awakened no general prejudice against him, for he was admitted into the best society and possessed immense wealth. Captain Murderer's mission was matrimony, and the gratification of a cannibal appetite with tender brides. On his marriage morning, he always caused both sides of the way to church to be planted with curious flowers; and when his bride said, "Dear Captain Murderer, I never saw flowers like these before: what are they called?" he answered, "They are called Garnish for house-lamb," and laughed at his ferocious practical joke in a horrid manner, disquieting the minds of the noble bridal company, with a very sharp show of teeth, then displayed for the first time. He made love in a coach and six, and married in a coach and twelve, and all his horses were milk-white horses with one red spot on the back which he caused to be hidden by the harness. For, the spot *would* come there, though every horse was milk-white when Captain Murderer bought him. And the spot was young bride's blood. (To this terrific point I am indebted for my first personal experience of a shudder and cold beads on the forehead.) When Captain Murderer had made an end of feasting and revelry, and had dismissed the noble guests, and was alone with his wife on the day month after their marriage, it was his whimsical custom to produce a golden rolling-pin and a silver pie-board. Now, there was this special feature in the Captain's courtships, that he always asked if the young lady could make pie-crust; and if she couldn't by nature or education, she was taught. Well. When the bride saw Captain Murderer produce the golden rolling-pin and silver pie-board, she remembered this, and turned up her laced-silk sleeves to make a pie. The Captain brought out a silver pie-dish of immense capacity, and the Captain brought out flour and butter and eggs and all things needful, except the inside of the pie; of materials for the staple of the pie itself, the Captain brought out none. Then said the lovely bride, "Dear Captain Murderer, what pie is this to be?" He replied, "A meat pie." Then said the lovely bride, "Dear Captain Murderer, I see no meat." The Captain humorously retorted, "Look in the glass." She looked in the glass, but still she saw no meat, and then the Captain roared with laughter, and, suddenly frowning and drawing his sword, bade her roll out the crust. So she rolled out the crust, dropping large tears upon it all the time because he was so cross, and when she had lined the dish with crust and had cut the crust all ready to fit the top, the Captain called out, "*I* see the meat in the glass!" And the bride looked up at the glass, just in time to see the Captain cutting her head off; and he chopped her in pieces, and peppered her, and salted her, and put her in the pie, and sent it to the baker's, and ate it all, and picked the bones.

Captain Murderer went on in this way, prospering exceedingly, until he came to choose a bride from two twin sisters, and at first didn't know which to choose. For, though one was fair and the other dark, they were both equally beautiful. But the fair twin loved him, and the dark twin hated him, so he chose the fair one. The dark twin would have prevented the marriage if she could, but she couldn't; however, on the night before it, much suspecting Captain Murderer, she stole out and climbed his garden wall, and looked in at his window through a chink in the shutter, and saw him having his teeth filed sharp. Next day she listened all day, and heard him make his joke about the house-lamb. And that day month, he had the paste rolled out, and cut the fair twin's head off, and chopped her in pieces, and peppered her, and salted her, and put her in the pie, and sent it to the baker's, and ate it all, and picked the bones.

Now, the dark twin had had her suspicions much increased by the filing of the Captain's teeth, and again by the house-lamb joke. Putting all things together when he gave out that her sister was dead, she divined the truth, and determined to be revenged. So, she went up to Captain Murderer's house, and knocked at the knocker and pulled at the bell, and when the Captain came to the door, said: "Dear Captain Murderer, marry me next, for I always loved you and was jealous of my sister." The Captain took it as a compliment, and made a polite answer, and the marriage was quickly arranged. On the night before it, the bride again climbed to his window, and again saw him having his teeth filed sharp. At this sight, she laughed such a terrible laugh, at the chink in the shutter, that the Captain's blood curdled, and he said: "I hope nothing has disagreed with me!" At that, she laughed again, a still more terrible laugh, and the shutter was opened and search made, but she was nimbly gone, and there was no one. Next day they went to church in the coach and twelve, and were married. And that day month, she rolled the pie-crust out, and Captain Murderer cut her head off, and chopped her in pieces, and peppered her, and salted her, and put her in the pie, and sent it to the baker's, and ate it all, and picked the bones.

But before she began to roll out the paste she had taken a deadly poison of a most awful character, distilled from toads' eyes and spiders' knees; and Captain Murderer had hardly picked her last bone, when he began to swell, and to turn blue, and to be all over spots, and to scream. And he went on swelling and turning bluer and being more all over spots and screaming, until he reached from floor to ceiling and from wall to wall; and then, at one o'clock in the morning, he blew up with a loud explosion. At the sound of it, all the milk-white horses in the stables broke their halters and went mad, and then they galloped over everybody in Captain Murderer's house (beginning with the family blacksmith who had filed his teeth) until the whole were dead, and then they galloped away.

Hundreds of times did I hear this legend of Captain Murderer, in my early youth, and added hundreds of times was there a mental compulsion upon me in bed, to peep in at his window as the dark twin peeped, and to revisit his horrible house, and look at him in his blue and spotty and screaming stage, as he reached from floor to ceiling and from wall to wall. The young woman who brought me acquainted with Captain Murderer, had a fiendish enjoyment of my terrors, and used to begin, I remember—as a sort of introductory overture—by clawing the air with both hands, and uttering a long low hollow groan. So acutely did I suffer from this ceremony in combination with this infernal Captain, that I sometimes used to plead I thought I was hardly strong enough and old enough to hear the story again just yet. But, she never spared me one word of it, and indeed commended the awful chalice to my lips as the only preservative known to science against "The Black Cat"—a weird and glaring-eyed supernatural Tom, who was reputed to prowl about the world by night, sucking the breath of infancy, and who was endowed with a special thirst (as I was given to understand) for mine.

This female bard—may she have been repaid my debt of obligation to her in the matter of nightmares and perspirations!—reappears in my memory as the daughter of a shipwright. Her name was Mercy, though she had none on me. There was something of a ship-building flavour in the following story. As it always recurs to me in a vague association with calomel pills, I believe it to have been reserved for dull nights when I was low with medicine.

There was once a shipwright, and he wrought in a Government Yard, and his name was Chips. And his father's name before him was Chips, and *his* father's name before *him* was Chips, and they were all Chipses. And Chips the father had sold himself to the Devil for an iron pot and a bushel of tenpenny nails and half a ton of copper and a rat that could speak; and Chips the grandfather had sold himself to the Devil for an iron pot and a bushel of tenpenny nails and half a ton of copper and a rat that could speak; and Chips the great-grandfather had disposed of himself in the same direction on the same terms; and the bargain had run in the family for a long long time. So, one day when young Chips was at work in the Dock Slip all alone, down in the dark hold of an old Seventy-four that was haled up for repairs, the Devil presented himself, and remarked:

> "A Lemon has pips,
> And a Yard has ships,
> And *I*'ll have Chips!"

(I don't know why, but this fact of the Devil's expressing himself in rhyme was peculiarly trying to me.) Chips looked up when he heard the words, and there he saw the Devil with saucer eyes that squinted on a terrible great scale, and that struck out sparks of blue fire continually. And whenever he winked his eyes, showers of blue sparks came out, and his eyelashes made a clattering like flints and steels striking lights. And hanging over one of his arms by the handle was an iron pot, and under that arm was a bushel of tenpenny nails, and under his other arm was half a ton of copper, and sitting on one of his shoulders was a rat that could speak. So, the Devil said again:

> "A Lemon has pips,
> And a Yard has ships,
> And *I*'ll have Chips!"

(The invariable effect of this alarming tautology on the part of the Evil Spirit was to deprive me of my senses for some moments.) So, Chips answered never a word, but went on with his work. "What are you doing, Chips?" said the rat that could speak. "I am putting in new planks where you and your gang have eaten old away," said Chips. "But we'll eat them too," said the rat that could speak; "and we'll let in the water and drown the crew, and we'll eat them too." Chips, being only a shipwright, and not a Man-of-war's man, said, "You are welcome to it." But he couldn't keep his eyes off the half a ton of copper or the bushel of tenpenny nails; for nails and copper are a shipwright's sweethearts, and shipwrights will run away with them whenever they can. So, the Devil said, "I see what you are looking at, Chips. You had better strike the bargain. You know the terms. Your father before you was well acquainted with them, and so were your grandfather and great-grandfather before him." Says Chips, "I like the copper, and I like the nails, and I don't mind the pot, but I don't like the rat." Says the Devil, fiercely, "You can't have the metal without him—and *he's* a curiosity. I'm going." Chips, afraid of losing the half a ton of copper and the bushel of nails, then said, "Give us hold!" So, he got the copper and the nails and the pot and the rat that could speak, and the Devil vanished. Chips sold the copper, and he sold the nails, and he would have sold the pot; but whenever he offered it for sale, the rat was in it, and the dealers dropped it, and would have nothing to say to the bargain. So, Chips resolved to kill the rat, and, being at work in the Yard one day with a great kettle of hot pitch on one side of him and the iron pot with the rat in it on the other, he turned the scalding pitch into the pot, and filled it full. Then, he kept his eye upon it till it cooled and hardened, and then he let it stand for twenty days, and then he heated the pitch again and turned it back into the kettle, and then he sank the pot in water for twenty days more, and then he got the smelters to put it in the furnace for twenty days more, and then they gave it him out, red hot, and looking like red-hot glass instead of iron—yet there was the rat in it, just the same as ever! And the moment it caught his eye, it said with a jeer:

> "A Lemon has pips,
> And a Yard has ships,
> And *I*'ll have Chips!"

(For this Refrain I had waited since its last appearance, with inexpressible horror, which now culminated.) Chips now felt certain in his own mind that the rat would stick to him; the rat, answering his thought, said, "I will—like pitch!"

Now, as the rat leaped out of the pot when it had spoken, and made off, Chips began to hope that it wouldn't keep its word. But, a terrible thing happened next day. For, when dinner-time came and the Dock-bell rang to strike work, he put his rule into the long pocket at the side of his trousers, and there he found a rat—not that rat, but another rat. And in his hat, he found another; and in his pocket-handkerchief, another; and in the sleeves of his coat, when he pulled it on to go to dinner, two more. And from that time he found himself so frightfully intimate with all the rats in the Yard, that they climbed up his legs when he was at work, and sat on his tools while he used them. And they could all speak to one another, and he understood what they said. And they got into his lodging, and into his bed, and into his teapot, and into his beer, and into his boots. And he was going to be married to a corn-chandler's daughter; and when he gave her a workbox he had himself made for her, a rat jumped out of it; and when he put his arm round her waist, a rat clung about her; so the marriage was broken off, though the banns were already twice put up—which the parish clerk well remembers, for, as he handed the book to the clergyman for the second time of asking, a large fat rat ran over the leaf. (By this time a special cascade of rats was rolling down my back; and the whole of my small listening person was overrun with them. At intervals ever since, I have been morbidly afraid of my own pocket, lest my exploring hand should find a specimen or two of those vermin in it.)

You may believe that all this was very terrible to Chips; but even all this was not the worst. He knew besides, what the rats were doing, wherever they were. So, sometimes he would cry aloud, when he was at his club at night, "Oh! Keep the rats out of the convicts' burying-ground! Don't let them do that!" Or, "There's one of them at the cheese down stairs!" Or, "There's two of them smelling at the baby in the garret!" Or, other things of that sort. At last, he was voted mad, and lost his work in the Yard, and could get no other work. But, King George wanted men, so before very long he got pressed for a sailor. And so he was taken off in a boat one evening to his ship, lying at Spithead, ready to sail. And so the first thing he made out in her as he got near her, was the figure-head of the old Seventy-four, where he had seen the Devil. She was called the Argonaut, and they rowed right under the bowsprit where the figure-head of the Argonaut, with a sheepskin in his hand and a blue gown on, was looking out to sea; and sitting staring on his forehead was the rat who could speak, and his exact words were these: "Chips ahoy! Old boy! We've pretty well eat them too, and we'll drown the crew, and will eat them too!" (Here I always became exceedingly faint, and would have asked for water, but that I was speechless.)

The ship was bound for the Indies; and if you don't know where that is, you ought to it, and angels will never love you. (Here I felt myself an outcast from a future state.) The ship set sail that very night, and she sailed, and sailed, and sailed. Chips's feelings were dreadful. Nothing ever equalled his terrors. No wonder. At last, one day he asked leave to speak to the Admiral. The Admiral giv' leave. Chips went down on his knees in the Great State Cabin. "Your Honour, unless your Honour, without a moment's loss of time makes sail for the nearest shore, this is a doomed ship, and her name is the Coffin!" "Young man, your words are a madman's words." "Your Honour no; they are nibbling us away." "They?" "Your Honour, them dreadful rats. Dust and hollowness where solid oak ought to be! Rats nibbling a grave for every man on board! Oh! Does your Honour love your Lady and your pretty children?" "Yes, my man, to be sure." "Then, for God's sake, make for the nearest shore, for at this present moment the rats are all stopping in their work, and are all looking straight towards you with bare teeth, and are all saying to one another that you shall never, never, never,

CHIPS AND THE ADMIRAL. 233

never, see your Lady and your children more." "My poor fellow, you are a case for the doctor. Sentry, take care of this man!"

So, he was bled and he was blistered, and he was this and that, for six whole days and nights. So, then he again asked leave to speak to the Admiral. The Admiral giv' leave. He went down on his knees in the Great State Cabin. "Now, Admiral, you must die! You took no warning; you must die! The rats are never wrong in their calculations, and they make out that they'll be through, at twelve to-night. So, you must die!—With me and all the rest!" And so at twelve o'clock there was a great leak reported in the ship, and a torrent of water rushed in and nothing could stop it, and they all went down, every living soul. And what the rats—being water-rats—left of Chips, at last floated to shore, and sitting on him was an immense overgrown rat, laughing, that dived when the corpse touched the beach and never came up. And there was a deal of seaweed on the remains. And if you get thirteen bits of seaweed, and dry them and burn them in the fire, they will go off like in these thirteen words as plain as plain can be:

> "A Lemon has pips,
> And a Yard has ships,
> And *I*'ve got Chips!"

The same female bard—descended, possibly, from those terrible old Scalds who seem to have existed for the express purpose of addling the brains of mankind when they begin to investigate languages—made a standing pretence which greatly assisted in forcing me back to a number of hideous places that I would by all means have avoided. This pretence was, that all her ghost stories had occurred to her own relations. Politeness towards a meritorious family, therefore forbade my doubting them, and they acquired an air of authentication that impaired my digestive powers for life. There was a narrative concerning an unearthly animal foreboding death, which appeared in the open street to a parlour-maid who "went to fetch the beer" for supper: first (as I now recal it) assuming the likeness of a black dog, and gradually rising on its hind-legs and swelling into the semblance of some quadruped greatly surpassing a hippopotamus: which apparition—not because I deemed it in the least improbable, but because I felt it to be really too large to bear—I feebly endeavoured to explain away. But, on Mercy's retorting with wounded dignity that the parlour-maid was her own sister-in-law, I perceived there was no hope, and resigned myself to this zoological phenomenon as one of my many pursuers. There was another narrative describing the apparition of a young woman who came out of a glass-case and haunted another young woman until the other young woman questioned it and elicited that its bones (Lord! To think of its being so particular about its bones!) were buried under the glass-case, whereas she required them to be interred, with every Undertaking solemnity up to twenty-four pound ten, in another particular place. This narrative I considered I had a personal interest in disproving, because we had glass-cases at home, and how, otherwise, was I to be guaranteed from the intrusion of young women requiring *me* to bury them up to twenty-four pound ten, when I had only twopence a week? But my remorseless nurse cut the ground from under my tender feet, by informing me that She was the other young woman; and I couldn't say "I don't believe you;" it was not possible.

Such are a few of the uncommercial journeys that I was forced to make, against my will, when I was very young and unreasoning. And really, as to the latter part of them, it is not so very long ago—now I come to think of it—that I was asked to undertake them once again, with a steady countenance.

XVI.

ARCADIAN LONDON.

BEING in a humour for complete solitude and uninterrupted meditation this autumn, I have taken a lodging for six weeks in the most unfrequented part of England—in a word, in London.

The retreat into which I have withdrawn myself, is Bond-street. From this lonely spot I make pilgrimages into the surrounding wilderness, and traverse extensive tracts of the Great Desert. The first solemn feeling of isolation overcome, the first oppressive consciousness of profound retirement conquered, I enjoy that sense of freedom, and feel reviving within me that latent wildness of the original savage, which has been (upon the whole somewhat frequently) noticed by Travellers.

My lodgings are at a hatter's—my own hatter's. After exhibiting no articles in his window for some weeks, but sea-side wide-awakes, shooting-caps, and a choice of rough waterproof head-gear for the moors and mountains, he has put upon the heads of his family as much of this stock as they could carry, and has taken them off to the Isle of Thanet. His young man alone remains—and remains alone—in the shop. The young man has let out the fire at which the irons are heated, and, saving his strong sense of duty, I see no reason why he should take the shutters down.

Happily for himself and for his country, the young man is a Volunteer; most happily for himself, or I think he would become the prey of a settled melancholy. For, to live surrounded by human hats, and alienated from human heads to fit them on, is surely a great endurance. But, the young man, sustained by practising his exercise, and by constantly furbishing up his regulation plume (it is unnecessary to observe that, as a hatter, he is in a cock's-feather corps), is resigned, and uncomplaining. On a Saturday, when he closes early and gets his Knickerbockers on, he is even cheerful. I am gratefully particular in this reference to him, because he is my companion through many peaceful hours. My hatter has a desk up certain steps behind his counter, enclosed like the clerk's desk at Church. I shut myself into this place of seclusion, after breakfast, and meditate. At such times, I observe the young man loading an imaginary rifle with the greatest precision, and maintaining a most galling and destructive fire upon the national enemy. I thank him publicly for his companionship and his patriotism.

The simple character of my life, and the calm nature of the scenes by which I am surrounded, occasion me to rise early. I go forth in my slippers, and promenade the pavement. It is pastoral to feel the freshness of the air in the uninhabited town, and to appreciate the shepherdess character of the few milkwomen who purvey so little milk that it would be worth nobody's while to adulterate it, if anybody were left to undertake the task. On the crowded sea-shore, the great demand for milk, combined with the strong local temptation of chalk, would betray itself in the lowered quality of the article. In Arcadian London, I derive it from the cow.

The Arcadian simplicity of the metropolis altogether, and the primitive ways into which it has fallen in this autumnal Golden Age, make it entirely new to me. Within a few hundred yards of my retreat, is the house of a friend who maintains a most sumptuous butler. I never, until yesterday, saw that butler out of superfine black broadcloth. Until yesterday, I never saw him off duty, never saw him (he is the best of butlers) with the appearance of having any mind for anything but the glory of his master and his master's friends. Yesterday morning, walking in my slippers near the house of which he is the prop and ornament—a house now a waste of shutters—I encountered that butler, also in his slippers, and in a shooting suit of one colour, and in a low-crowned straw hat, smoking an early cigar. He felt that we had formerly met in another state of existence, and that we were translated into a new sphere. Wisely and well, he passed me without recognition. Under his arm he carried the morning paper, and shortly afterwards I saw him sitting on a rail in the pleasant open landscape of Regent-street, perusing it at his ease under the ripening sun.

My landlord having taken his whole establishment to

be salted down, I am waited on by an elderly woman labouring under a chronic sniff, who, at the shadowy hour of half-past nine o'clock of every evening, gives admittance at the street door to a meagre and mouldy old man whom I have never yet seen detached from a flat pint of beer in a pewter pot. The meagre and mouldy old man is her husband, and the pair have a dejected consciousness that they are not justified in appearing on the surface of the earth. They come out of some hole when London empties itself, and go in again when it fills. I saw them arrive on the evening when I myself took possession, and they arrived with the flat pint of beer, and their bed in a bundle. The old man is a weak old man, and appeared to me to get the bed down the kitchen stairs by tumbling down with and upon it. They make their bed in the lowest and remotest corner of the basement, and they smell of bed, and have no possession but bed: unless it be (which I rather infer from an under-current of flavour in them) cheese. I know their name, through the chance of having called the wife's attention, at half-past nine on the second evening of our acquaintance, to the circumstance of there being some one at the house door; when she apologetically explained, "It's on'y Mr. Klem." What becomes of Mr. Klem all day, or when he goes out, or why, is a mystery I cannot penetrate; but at half-past nine he never fails to turn up on the door-step with the flat pint of beer. And the pint of beer, flat as it is, is so much more important than himself, that it always seems to my fancy as if it had found him drivelling in the street and had humanely brought him home. In making his way below, Mr. Klem never goes down the middle of the passage, like another Christian, but shuffles against the wall as if entreating me to take notice that he is occupying as little space as possible in the house; and whenever I come upon him face to face, he backs from me in fascinated confusion. The most extraordinary circumstance I have traced in connexion with this aged couple, is, that there is a Miss Klem, their daughter, apparently ten years older than either of them, who has also a bed and smells of it, and carries it about the earth at dusk and hides it in deserted houses. I came into this piece of knowledge through Mrs. Klem's beseeching me to sanction the sheltering of Miss Klem under that roof for a single night, "between her takin' care of the upper part in Pall Mall which the family of his back, and a 'ouse in Serjameses-street, which the family of leaves towng termorrer." I gave my gracious consent (having nothing that I know of to do with it), and in the shadowy hours Miss Klem became perceptible on the door-step, wrestling with a bed in a bundle. Where she made it up for the night I cannot positively state, but, I think, in a sink. I know that with the instinct of a reptile or an insect, she stowed it and herself away in deep obscurity. In the Klem family, I have noticed another remarkable gift of nature, and that is a power they possess of converting everything into flue. Such broken victuals as they take by stealth, appear (whatever the nature of the viands) invariably to generate flue; and even the nightly pint of beer, instead of assimilating naturally, strikes me as breaking out in that form, equally on the shabby gown of Mrs. Klem, and the threadbare coat of her husband.

Mrs. Klem has no idea of my name—as to Mr. Klem, he has no idea of anything—and only knows me as her good gentleman. Thus, if doubtful whether I am in my room or no, Mrs. Klem taps at the door and says, "Is my good gentleman here?" Or, if a messenger desiring to see me were consistent with my solitude, she would show him in with "Here is my good gentleman." I find this to be a generic custom. For, I meant to have observed before now, that in its Arcadian time all my part of London is indistinctly pervaded by the Klem species. They creep about with beds, and go to bed in miles of deserted houses. They hold no companionship, except that sometimes, after dark, two of them will emerge from opposite houses, and meet in the middle of the road as on neutral ground, or will peep from adjoining houses over an interposing barrier of area railings, and compare a few reserved mistrustful notes respecting their good ladies or good gentlemen. This I have discovered in the course of various solitary rambles I have taken Northward from my retirement, along the awful perspectives of Wimpole-street, Harley-street, and similar frowning regions. Their effect would be scarcely distinguishable from that of the primeval forests, but for the Klem stragglers; these may be dimly observed, when the heavy shadows fall, flitting to and fro, putting up the door-chain, taking in the pint of beer, lowering like phantoms at the dark parlour windows, or secretly consorting underground with the dust-bin and the water-cistern.

In the Burlington Arcade, I observe, with peculiar pleasure, a primitive state of manners to have superseded the baneful influences of ultra civilisation. Nothing can surpass the innocence of the ladies' shoe-shops, the artificial flower repositories, and the head-dress depôts. They are in strange hands at this time of year—hands of unaccustomed persons, who are imperfectly acquainted with the prices of the goods, and contemplate them with unsophisticated delight and wonder. The children of these virtuous people exchange familiarities in the Arcade, and temper the asperity of the two tall beadles. Their youthful prattle blends in an unwonted manner with the harmonious shade of the scene, and the general effect is, as of the voices of birds in a grove. In this happy restoration of the golden time, it has been my privilege even to see the bigger beadle's wife. She brought him his dinner in a basin, and he ate it in his arm-chair, and afterwards fell asleep like a satiated child. At Mr. Truefitt's, the excellent hairdresser's, they are learning French to beguile the time; and even the few solitaries left on guard at Mr. Atkinson's, the perfumer's round the corner (generally the most inexorable gentlemen in London, and the most scornful of three-and-sixpence), condescend a little as they drowsily bide or recal their turn for chasing the ebbing Neptune on the ribbed seasand. From Messrs. Hunt and Roskell's, the jewellers, all things are absent but the precious stones, and the gold and silver, and the soldierly pensioner at the door with his decorated breast. I might stand night and day for a month to come, in Saville-row, with my tongue out, yet not find a doctor to look at it for love or money. The dentists' instruments are rusting in their drawers, and their horrible cool parlours, where people pretend to read the Every-Day Book and not to be afraid, are doing penance for their grimness in white sheets. The light-weight of shrewd appearance, with one eye always shut up, as if he were eating a sharp gooseberry in all seasons, who usually stands at the gateway of the livery stables on very little legs under a very large waistcoat, has gone to Doncaster. Of such undesigning aspect is his guileless Yard now, with its gravel and scarlet beans, and the yellow Break housed under a glass roof in a corner, that I almost believe I could not be taken in there, if I tried. In the places of business of the great tailors, the cheval-glasses are dim and dusty for lack of being looked into. Ranges of brown paper coat and waistcoat bodies look as funereal as if they were the hatchments of the customers with whose names they are inscribed; the measuring tapes hang idle on the wall; the order-taker, left on the hopeless chance of some one looking in, yawns in the last extremity over the books of patterns, as if he were trying to read that entertaining library. The hotels in Brook-street have no one in them, and the staffs of servants stare disconsolately for next season out of all the windows. The very man who goes about like an erect Turtle, between two boards recommendatory of the Sixteen Shilling Trousers, is aware of himself as a hollow mockery, and eats filberts while he leans his hinder shell against a wall.

Among these tranquillising objects, it is my delight to walk and meditate. Soothed by the repose around me, I wander insensibly to considerable distances, and guide myself back by the stars. Thus, I enjoy the contrast of a few still partially inhabited and busy spots where all the lights are not fled, where all the garlands are not dead, whence all but I have not departed. Then, does it appear to me that in this age three things are clamorously required of Man in the miscellaneous thoroughfares of the metropolis. Firstly, that he have his boots cleaned. Secondly, that he eat a penny ice. Thirdly, that he get himself photographed. Then do I speculate, What have those seam-worn artists been who stand at the photograph doors in Greek caps, sample in hand, and mysteriously salute the public—the female public with a pressing tenderness—to come in and be "took"? What did they do with their greasy blandishments, before the era of cheap photography? Of what class were their previous victims, and how victimised? And how did they get, and how did they pay for, that large collection of likenesses, all purporting to have been taken inside, with the taking of none of which had that establishment any more to do than with the taking of Delhi?

But, these are small oases, and I am soon back again in metropolitan Arcadia. It is my impression that much of its serene and peaceful character is attributable to the absence of customary Talk. How do I know but there may be subtle influences in Talk, to vex the souls of men who don't hear it? How do I know but that Talk, five, ten, twenty miles off, may get into the air and disagree with

me? If I rise from my bed, vaguely troubled and wearied
and sick of my life, in the session of Parliament, who
shall say that my noble friend, my right reverend friend,
my right honourable friend, my honourable friend, my
honourable and learned friend, or my honourable and
gallant friend, may not be responsible for that effect
upon my nervous system? Too much Ozone in the air,
I am informed and fully believe (though I have no idea
what it is), would affect me in a marvellously disagreeable way; why may not too much Talk? I don't see or
hear the Ozone; I don't see or hear the Talk. And
there is so much Talk; so much too much; such loud
cry, and such scant supply of wool; such a deal of
fleecing, and so little fleece! Hence, in the Arcadian
season, I find it a delicious triumph to walk down to deserted Westminster, and see the Courts shut up; to walk
a little further and see the Two Houses shut up; to
stand in the Abbey Yard, like the New Zealander of the
grand English History (concerning which unfortunate
man, a whole rookery of mares' nests is generally being discovered), and gloat upon the ruins of Talk. Returning
to my primitive solitude and lying down to sleep, my
grateful heart expands with the consciousness that there
is no adjourned Debate, no ministerial explanation,
nobody to give notice of intention to ask the noble Lord
at the head of her Majesty's Government five-and-twenty
bootless questions in one, no term time with legal argu-
ment, no Nisi Prius with eloquent appeal to British
Jury; that the air will to-morrow, and to-morrow, and
to-morrow, remain untroubled by this superabundant

generating of Talk. In a minor degree it is a delicious triumph to me to go into the club, and see the carpets up, and the Bores and the other dust dispersed to the four winds. Again New Zealander-like, I stand on the cold hearth, and say in the solitude, "Here I watched Bore A 1, with voice always mysteriously low and head always mysteriously drooped, whispering political secrets into the ears of Adam's confiding children. Accursed be his memory for ever and a day!"

But, I have all this time been coming to the point, that the happy nature of my retirement is most sweetly expressed in its being the abode of Love. It is, as it were, an inexpensive Agapemone: nobody's speculation: everybody's profit. The one great result of the resumption of primitive habits, and (convertible terms) the not having much to do, is, the abounding of Love.

The Klem species are incapable of the softer emotions; probably, in that low nomadic race, the softer emotions have all degenerated into flue. But, with this exception, all the sharers of my retreat make love.

I have mentioned Saville-row. We all know the Doctor's servant. We all know what a respectable man he is, what a hard dry man, what a firm man, what a confidential man: how he lets us into the waiting-room, like a man who knows minutely what is the matter with us, but from whom the rack should not wring the secret. In the prosaic "season," he has distinctly the appearance of a man conscious of money in the savings bank, and taking his stand on his respectability with both feet. At that time it is as impossible to associate him with relaxation, or any human weakness, as it is to meet his eye without feeling guilty of indisposition. In the blest Arcadian time, how changed! I have seen him, in a pepper-and-salt jacket—jacket—and drab trousers, with his arm round the waist of a bootmaker's housemaid, smiling in open day. I have seen him at the pump by the Albany, unsolicitedly pumping for two fair young creatures, whose figures as they bent over their cans, were—if I may be allowed an original expression—a model for the sculptor. I have seen him trying the piano in the Doctor's drawing-room with his forefinger, and have heard him humming tunes in praise of lovely woman. I have seen him seated on a fire-engine, and going (obviously in search of excitement) to a fire. I saw him, one moonlight evening when the peace and purity of our Arcadian west were at their height, polk with the lovely daughter of a cleaner of gloves, from the door-steps of his own residence, across Saville-row, round by Clifford-street and Old Burlington-street, back to Burlington-gardens. Is this the Golden Age revived, or Iron London?

The Dentist's servant. Is that man no mystery to us, no type of invisible power? The tremendous individual knows (who else does?) what is done with the extracted teeth; he knows what goes on in the little room where something is always being washed or filed; he knows what warm spicy infusion is put into the comfortable tumbler from which we rinse our wounded mouth, with a gap in it that feels a foot wide; he knows whether the thing we spit into is a fixture communicating with the Thames, or could be cleared away for a dance; he sees the horrible parlour when there are no patients in it, and he could reveal, if he would, what becomes of the Every-Day Book then. The conviction of my coward conscience when I see that man in a professional light, is, that he knows all the statistics of my teeth and gums, my double teeth, my single teeth, my stopped teeth, and my sound. In this Arcadian rest, I am fearless of him as of a harmless powerless creature in a Scotch cap, who adores a young lady in a voluminous crinoline, at a neighbouring billiard-room, and whose passion would be uninfluenced if every one of her teeth were false. They may be. He takes them all on trust.

In secluded corners of the place of my seclusion, there are little shops withdrawn from public curiosity, and never two together, where servants' perquisites are bought. The cook may dispose of grease at these modest and convenient marts; the butler, of bottles; the valet and lady's maid, of clothes; most servants, indeed, of most things they may happen to lay hold of. I have been told that in sterner times loving correspondence otherwise interdicted may be maintained by letter through the agency of some of these useful establishments. In the Arcadian autumn, no such device is necessary. Everybody loves, and openly and blamelessly loves. My landlord's young man loves the whole of one side of the way of old Bond-street, and is beloved several doors up new Bond-street besides. I never look out of window but I see kissing of hands going on all around me. It is the morning custom to glide from shop to shop and exchange tender sentiments; it is the evening custom for couples to stand hand in hand at house doors, or roam, linked in that flowery manner, through the unpeopled streets. There is nothing else to do but love; and what there is to do, is done.

In unison with this pursuit, a chaste simplicity obtains in the domestic habits of Arcadia. Its few scattered people dine early, live moderately, sup socially, and sleep soundly. It is rumoured that the Beadles of the Arcade, from being the mortal enemies of boys, have signed with tears an address to Lord Shaftesbury, and subscribed to a ragged school. No wonder! For, they might turn their heavy maces into crooks and tend sheep in the Arcade, to the purling of the water-carts as they give the thirsty streets much more to drink than they can carry.

A happy Golden Age, and a serene tranquillity. Charming picture, but it will fade. The iron age will return, London will come back to town, if I show my tongue then in Saville-row for half a minute I shall be prescribed for, the Doctor's man and the Dentist's man will then pretend that these days of unprofessional innocence never existed. Where Mr. and Mrs. Klem and their bed will be at that time, passes human knowledge; but, my hatter hermitage will then know them no more, nor will it then know me. The desk at which I have written these meditations will retributively assist at the making out of my account, and the wheels of gorgeous carriages and the hoofs of high-stepping horses will crush the silence out of Bond-street—will grind Arcadia away, and give it to the elements in granite powder.

XVII.

THE ITALIAN PRISONER.

The rising of the Italian people from under their unutterable wrongs, and the tardy burst of day upon them after the long long night of oppression that has darkened their beautiful country, has naturally caused my mind to dwell often of late on my own small wanderings in Italy. Connected with them, is a curious little drama, in which the character I myself sustained was so very subordinate, that I may relate its story without any fear of being suspected of self-display. It is strictly a true story.

I am newly arrived one summer evening, in a certain small town on the Mediterranean. I have had my dinner at the inn, and I and the mosquitoes are coming out into the streets together. It is far from Naples; but a bright brown plump little woman-servant at the inn, is a Neapolitan, and is so vivaciously expert in pantomimic action, that in the single moment of answering my request to have a pair of shoes cleaned which I have left up-stairs, she plies imaginary brushes, and goes completely through the motions of polishing the shoes up, and laying them at my feet. I smile at the brisk little woman in perfect satisfaction with her briskness; and the brisk little woman, amiably pleased with me because I am pleased with her, claps her hands and laughs delightfully. We are in the inn yard. As the little woman's bright eyes sparkle on the cigarette I am smoking I make bold to offer her one; she accepts it none the less merrily, because I touch a most charming little dimple in her fat cheek, with its light paper end. Glancing up at the many green lattices to assure herself that the mistress is not looking on, the little woman then puts her two little dimpled arms a-kimbo, and stands on tiptoe to light her cigarette at mine. "And now, dear little sir," says she, puffing out smoke in a most innocent and Cherubic manner, "keep quite straight on, take the first to the right, and probably you will see him standing at his door."

I have a commission to "him," and I have been inquiring about him. I have carried the commission about Italy, several months. Before I left England, there came to me one night a certain generous and gentle English nobleman (he is dead in these days when I relate the story, and exiles have lost their best British friend), with this request: "Whenever you come to such a town, will you seek out one Giovanni Carlavero, who keeps a little wine-shop there, mention my name to him suddenly, and observe how it affects him?" I accepted the trust, and am on my way to discharge it.

The sirocco has been blowing all day, and it is a hot unwholesome evening with no cool sea-breeze. Mosquitoes and fire-flies are lively enough, but most other creatures are faint. The coquettish airs of pretty young women in the tiniest and wickedest of dolls' straw hats, who lean out at opened lattice blinds, are almost the only airs stirring. Very ugly and haggard old women with distaffs, and with a grey tow upon them that looks as if they were spinning out their own hair (I suppose they were once pretty, too, but it is very difficult to believe so), sit on the footway leaning against house walls. Everybody who has come for water to the fountain, stays there, and seems incapable of any such energetic idea as going home. Vespers are over, though not so long but that I can smell the heavy resinous incense as I pass the church. No man seems to be at work, save the coppersmith. In an Italian town he is always at work, and always thumping in the deadliest manner.

I keep straight on, and come in due time to the first on the right: a narrow dull street, where I see a well-favoured man of good stature and military bearing, in a great cloak, standing at a door. Drawing nearer to this threshold, I see it is the threshold of a small wine-shop; and I can just make out, in the dim light, the inscription that it is kept by Giovanni Carlavero.

I touch my hat to the figure in the cloak, and pass in, and draw a stool to a little table. The lamp (just such another as they dig out of Pompeii) is lighted, but the place is empty. The figure in the cloak has followed me in, and stands before me.

"The master?"

"At your service, sir."

"Please to give me a glass of the wine of the country."

He turns to a little counter, to get it. As his striking face is pale, and his action is evidently that of an enfeebled man, I remark that I fear he has been ill. It is not much, he courteously and gravely answers, though bad while it lasts: the fever.

As he sets the wine on the little table, to his manifest surprise I lay my hand on the back of his, look him in the face, and say in a low voice: "I am an Englishman, and you are acquainted with a friend of mine. Do you recollect ——?" and I mention the name of my generous countryman.

Instantly, he utters a loud cry, bursts into tears, and falls on his knees at my feet, clasping my legs in both his arms and bowing his head to the ground.

Some years ago, this man at my feet, whose overfraught heart is heaving as if it would burst from his breast, and whose tears are wet upon the dress I wear, was a galley-slave in the North of Italy. He was a political offender, having been concerned in the then last rising, and was sentenced to imprisonment for life. That he would have died in his chains, is certain, but for the circumstance that the Englishman happened to visit his prison.

It was one of the vile old prisons of Italy, and a part of it was below the waters of the harbour. The place of his confinement was an arched underground and underwater gallery, with a grill-gate at the entrance, through which it received such light and air as it got. Its condition was insufferably foul, and a stranger could hardly breathe in it, or see in it with the aid of a torch. At the upper end of this dungeon, and consequently in the worst position, as being the furthest removed from light and air, the Englishman first beheld him, sitting on an iron bedstead to which he was chained by a heavy chain. His countenance impressed the Englishman as having nothing in common with the faces of the malefactors with whom he was associated, and he talked with him, and learnt how he came to be there.

When the Englishman emerged from the dreadful den into the light of day, he asked his conductor, the governor of the jail, why Giovanni Carlavero was put into the worst place?

"Because he is particularly recommended," was the stringent answer.

"Recommended, that is to say, for death?"

"Excuse me; particularly recommended," was again the answer.

"He has a bad tumour in his neck, no doubt occasioned by the hardship of his miserable life. If it continues to be neglected, and he remains where he is, it will kill him."

"Excuse me, I can do nothing. He is particularly recommended."

The Englishman was staying in that town, and he went to his home there; but the figure of this man chained to the bedstead made it no home, and destroyed his rest and peace. He was an Englishman of an extraordinarily tender heart, and he could not bear the picture. He went back to the prison grate; went back again and again, and talked to the man and cheered him. He used his utmost influence to get the man unchained from the bedstead, were it only for ever so short a time in the day, and permitted to come to the grate. It took a long time, but the Englishman's station, personal character, and steadiness of purpose, wore out opposition so far, and that grace was at last accorded. Through the bars, when he could thus get light upon the tumour, the Englishman lanced it, and it did well, and healed. His strong interest in the prisoner had greatly increased by this time, and he formed the desperate resolution that he would exert his utmost self-devotion and use his utmost efforts, to get Carlavero pardoned.

If the prisoner had been a brigand and a murderer, if he had committed every non-political crime in the Newgate Calendar and out of it, nothing would have been easier than for a man of any court or priestly influence to obtain his release. As it was, nothing could have been more difficult. Italian authorities, and English authorities who had interest with them, alike assured the Englishman that his object was hopeless. He met with nothing but evasion, refusal, and ridicule. His political prisoner became a joke in the place. It was especially observable that English Circumlocution, and English Society on its travels, were as humorous on the subject as Circumlocution and Society may be on any subject without loss of caste. But, the Englishman possessed (and proved it well in his life) a courage very uncommon among us: he had not the least fear of being considered a bore, in a good humane cause. So he went on persistently trying, and trying, and trying, to get Giovanni Carlavero out. That prisoner had been rigorously rechained, after the tumour operation, and it was not likely that his miserable life could last very long.

One day, when all the town knew about the Englishman and his political prisoner, there came to the Englishman, a certain sprightly Italian Advocate of whom he had some knowledge; and he made this strange proposal. "Give me a hundred pounds to obtain Carlavero's release. I think I can get him a pardon, with that money. But I cannot tell you what I am going to do with the money, nor must you ever ask me the question if I succeed, nor must you ever ask me for an account of the money if I fail." The Englishman decided to hazard the hundred pounds. He did so, and heard not another word of the matter. For half a year and more, the Advocate made no sign, and never once "took on" in any way, to have the subject on his mind. The Englishman was then obliged to change his residence to another and more famous town in the North of Italy. He parted from the poor prisoner with a sorrowful heart, as from a doomed man for whom there was no release but Death.

The Englishman lived in his new place of abode another half-year and more, and had no tidings of the wretched prisoner. At length, one day, he received from the Advocate a cool concise mysterious note, to this effect. "If you still wish to bestow that benefit upon the man in whom you were once interested, send me fifty pounds more, and I think it can be ensured." Now, the Englishman had long settled in his mind that the Advocate was a heartless sharper, who had preyed upon his credulity and his interest in an unfortunate sufferer. So, he sat down and wrote a dry answer, giving the Advocate to understand that he was wiser now than he had been formerly, and that no more money was extractable from his pocket.

He lived outside the city gates, some mile or two from the post-office, and was accustomed to walk into the city with his letters and post them himself. On a lovely spring day, when the sky was exquisitely blue, and the sea Divinely beautiful, he took his usual walk, carrying this letter to the Advocate in his pocket. As he went along, his gentle heart was much moved by the loveliness of the prospect, and by the thought of the slowly-dying prisoner chained to the bedstead, for whom the universe had no delights. As he drew nearer and nearer to the city where he was to post the letter, he became very uneasy in his mind. He debated with himself, was it remotely possible, after all, that this sum of fifty pounds could restore the fellow-creature whom he pitied so much, and for whom he had striven so hard, to liberty? He was not a conventionally rich Englishman—very far from that—but, he had a spare fifty pounds at the banker's. He resolved to risk it. Without doubt, GOD has recompensed him for the resolution.

He went to the banker's, and got a bill for the amount, and enclosed it in a letter to the Advocate that I wish I could have seen. He simply told the Advocate that he was quite a poor man, and that he was sensible it might be a great weakness in him to part with so much money on the faith of so vague a communication; but, that there it was, and that he prayed the Advocate to make a good use of it. If he did otherwise no good could ever come of it, and it would lie heavy on his soul one day.

Within a week, the Englishman was sitting at his breakfast, when he heard some suppressed sounds of agitation on the staircase, and Giovanni Carlavero leaped into the room and fell upon his breast, a free man!

Conscious of having wronged the Advocate in his own thoughts, the Englishman wrote him an earnest and grateful letter, avowing the fact, and entreating him to confide by what means and through what agency he had succeeded so well. The Advocate returned for answer through the post. "There are many things, as you know, in this Italy of ours, that are safest and best not even spoken of—far less written of. We may meet some day, and then I may tell you what you want to know; not here, and now." But, the two never did meet again. The Advocate was dead when the Englishman gave me my trust; and how the man had been set free, remained as great a mystery to the Englishman, and to the man himself, as it was to me.

But, I knew this:—here was the man, this sultry night, on his knees at my feet, because I was the Englishman's friend; here were his tears upon my dress; here were his sobs choking his utterance; here were his kisses on my hands, because they had touched the hands that had worked out his release. He had no need to tell me it would be happiness to him to die for his benefactor;

I doubt if I ever saw real, sterling, fervent gratitude of soul, before or since.

He was much watched and suspected, he said, and had had enough to do to keep himself out of trouble. This, and his not having prospered in his worldly affairs, had led to his having failed in his usual communications to the Englishman for—as I now remember the period—some two or three years. But, his prospects were brighter, and his wife who had been very ill had recovered, and his fever had left him, and he had bought a little vineyard, and would I carry to his benefactor the first of its wine? Ay, that I would (I told him with enthusiasm), and not a drop of it should be spilled or lost!

He had cautiously closed the door before speaking of himself, and had talked with such excess of emotion, and in a provincial Italian so difficult to understand, that I had more than once been obliged to stop him, and beg him to have compassion on me and be slower and calmer. By degrees he became so, and tranquilly walked back with me to the hotel. There, I sat down before I went to bed and wrote a faithful account of him to the Englishman: which I concluded by saying that I would bring the wine home, against any difficulties, every drop.

Early next morning when I came out at the hotel door to pursue my journey, I found my friend waiting with one of those immense bottles in which the Italian peasants store their wine—a bottle holding some half-dozen gallons—bound round with basket-work for greater safety on the journey. I see him now, in the bright sunlight, tears of gratitude in his eyes, proudly inviting my attention to this corpulent bottle. (At the street-corner hard by, two high-flavoured able-bodied monks—pretending to talk together, but keeping their four evil eyes upon us.)

How the bottle had been got there, did not appear; but, the difficulty of getting it into the ramshackle vetturino carriage in which I was departing, was so great, and it took up so much room when it was got in, that I elected to sit outside. The last I saw of Giovanni Carlavero was his running through the town by the side of the jingling wheels, clasping my hand as I stretched it down from the box, charging me with a thousand last loving and dutiful messages to his dear patron, and finally looking in at the bottle as it reposed inside, with an admiration of its honourable way of travelling that was beyond measure delightful.

And now, what disquiet of mind this dearly-beloved and highly-treasured Bottle began to cost me, no man knows. It was my precious charge through a long tour, and, for hundreds of miles, I never had it off my mind by day or by night. Over bad roads—and they were many—I clung to it with affectionate desperation. Up mountains, I looked in at it and saw it helplessly tilting over on its back, with terror. At innumerable inn doors when the weather was bad, I was obliged to be put into my vehicle before the Bottle could be got in, and was obliged to have the Bottle lifted out before human aid could come near me. The Imp of the same name, except that his associations were all evil and these associations were all good, would have been a less troublesome travelling companion. I might have served Mr. Cruikshank as a subject for a new illustration of the miseries of the Bottle. The National Temperance Society might have made a powerful Tract of me.

The suspicions that attached to this innocent Bottle, greatly aggravated my difficulties. It was like the apple-pie in the child's book. Parma pouted at it, Modena mocked it, Tuscany tackled it, Naples nibbled it, Rome refused it, Austria accused it, Soldiers suspected it, Jesuits jobbed it. I composed a neat Oration, developing my inoffensive intentions in connexion with this Bottle, and delivered it in an infinity of guard-houses, at a multitude of town gates, and on every drawbridge, angle, and rampart, of a complete system of fortifications. Fifty times a day, I got down to harangue an infuriated soldiery about the Bottle. Through the filthy degradation of the abject and vile Roman States, I had as much difficulty in working my way with the Bottle, as if it had bottled up a complete system of heretical theology. In the Neapolitan country, where everybody was a spy, a soldier, a priest, or a lazzarone, the shameless beggars of all four denominations incessantly pounced on the Bottle and made it a pretext for extorting money from me. Quires—quires do I say? Reams—of forms illegibly printed on whity-brown paper were filled up about the Bottle, and it was the subject of more stamping and sanding than I had ever seen before. In consequence of which haze of sand, perhaps, it was always irregular, and always latent with dismal penalties of going back or not going forward, which were only to be abated by the silver crossing of a base hand, poked shirtless out of a ragged uniform sleeve. Under all discouragements, however, I stuck to my Bottle, and held firm to my resolution that every drop of its contents should reach the Bottle's destination.

The latter refinement cost me a separate heap of troubles on its own separate account. What corkscrews did I see the military power bring out against that Bottle: what gimlets, spikes, divining rods, gauges, and unknown tests and instruments! At some places, they persisted in declaring that the wine must not be passed, without being opened and tasted; I, pleading to the contrary, used then to argue the question seated on the Bottle lest they should open it in spite of me. In the southern parts of Italy, more violent shrieking, face-making, and gesticulating, greater vehemence of speech and countenance and action, went on about that Bottle, than would attend fifty murders in a northern latitude. It raised important functionaries out of their beds, in the dead of night. I have known half a dozen military lanterns to disperse themselves at all points of a great sleeping Piazza, each lantern summoning some official creature to get up, put on his cocked-hat instantly, and come and stop the Bottle. It was characteristic that while this innocent Bottle had such immense difficulty in getting from little town to town, Signor Mazzini and the fiery cross were traversing Italy from end to end.

Still, I stuck to my Bottle, like any fine old English gentleman all of the olden time. The more the Bottle was interfered with, the stauncher I became (if possible) in my first determination that my countryman should have it delivered to him intact, as the man whom he had so nobly restored to life and liberty had delivered it to me. If ever I had been obstinate in my days—and I may have been, say, once or twice—I was obstinate about the Bottle. But, I made it a rule always to keep a pocket full of small coin at its service, and never to be out of temper in its cause. Thus, I and the Bottle made our way. Once, we had a break-down; rather a bad break-down, on a steep high place with the sea below us, on a tempestuous evening when it blew great guns. We were driving four wild horses abreast, Southern fashion, and there was some little difficulty in stopping them. I was outside, and not thrown off; but no words can describe my feelings when I saw the Bottle—travelling inside, as usual—burst the door open, and roll obesely out into the road. A blessed Bottle with a charmed existence, he took no hurt; and we repaired damage, and went on triumphant.

A thousand representations were made to me that the Bottle must be left at this place, or that, and called for again. I never yielded to one of them, and never parted from the Bottle, on any pretence, consideration, threat, or entreaty. I had no faith in any official receipt for the Bottle, and nothing would induce me to accept one. These unmanageable politics at last brought me and the Bottle, still triumphant, to Genoa. There, I took a tender and reluctant leave of him for a few weeks, and consigned him to a trusty English captain, to be conveyed to the Port of London by sea.

While the Bottle was on his voyage to England, I read the Shipping Intelligence as anxiously as if I had been an underwriter. There was some stormy weather after I myself had got to England by way of Switzerland and France, and my mind greatly misgave me that the Bottle might be wrecked. At last to my great joy, I received notice of his safe arrival, and immediately went down to Saint Katharine's Docks, and found him in a state of honourable captivity in the Custom House.

The wine was mere vinegar when I set it down before the generous Englishman—probably it had been something like vinegar when I took it up from Giovanni Carlavero—but not a drop of it was spilled or gone. And the Englishman told me, with much emotion in his face and voice, that he had never tasted wine that seemed to him so sweet and sound. And long afterwards, the Bottle graced his table. And the last time I saw him in this world that misses him, he took me aside in a crowd, to say, with his amiable smile: "We were talking of you only to-day at dinner, and I wished you had been there, for I had some claret up in Carlavero's Bottle."

THE END.

www.ingramcontent.com/pod-product-compliance
Lightning Source LLC
Chambersburg PA
CBHW032005230426
43672CB00010B/2261